PROMENADES

PROMENADES

✤

A Historian's Appreciation of
Modern French Literature

✤

RICHARD COBB

Oxford New York

OXFORD UNIVERSITY PRESS

1986

Oxford University Press, Walton Street, Oxford OX2 6DP

Oxford New York Toronto
Delhi Bombay Calcutta Madras Karachi
Petaling Jaya Singapore Hong Kong Tokyo
Nairobi Dar es Salaam Cape Town
Melbourne Auckland

and associated companies in
Beirut Berlin Ibadan Nicosia

Oxford is a trade mark of Oxford University Press

First published 1980 by Oxford University Press
First published as an Oxford University Press paperback 1986

British Library Cataloguing in Publication Data
Cobb, Richard
Promenades: a historian's appreciation of modern
French literature.
1. French fiction—20th century—History and
criticism   2. France in literature   3. France—
Social life and customs—20th century
I. Title
843'912'0932   PQ671
ISBN 0–19–283061–9

Printed in Great Britain

For my sister, Diana,
in gratitude for a happy childhood
in Frinton (4th Avenue),
Tunbridge Wells (eventually at 5A),
The Hythe (St. Leonard's House),
and, later, for happy stays
at Hemingford Abbots (the Old Cross Keys)
and Bedford

Contents

Introduction

'*Merci, m'sieu,*' said the little boy rather elaborately as I handed him his clockwork *Normandie*, which I had retrieved from the cloudy bottom of le Grand Bassin, a veritable graveyard of shipping. I was standing, in my Shrewsbury blue suit, with the warmish water up to my middle, in the round central pool of the Tuileries, into which I had fallen in an endeavour to fish out France's blue ribbon liner, the pride of *la Transat*, with the help of a folding-chair. When I had clambered back on shore, my suit steaming in the June sun, over the rim of this busy inland sea, the little boy, who was wearing a peaked cap with the anchors of the Marine Marchande on the front, thanked me again and stretched out his hand to my wet and weedy one. I retreated, my back to a concerned concert of worried solicitude from children and accompanying grown-ups: '*M'sieu, attention à ne pas prendre froid,*' in a cloud of steam that followed me throughout the gardens, but that fortunately had started to diminish by the time I reached the rue de la Paix.

When I was on holiday in Saint-Germain-de-la-Coudre, a village in the Orne not far from la Ferté-Bernard and Mamers, I spent much of my time playing with the local children among the willows lining the little stream that, further up, ran behind the houses on the main street and beneath the wooden lavatories that had been built out, as at the end of small landing-places, above it, each with a hole in the seat through which one could watch the eddies and the halting progress of leaves and bits of wood caught in the swift flow. Some of the village boys wore wooden clogs, without socks, others, heavy boots, over long black stockings; and, in the week, they were never out of their shiny, billowing black tunics, with puffed, Laudian sleeves. They too were elaborately formal, displaying a politeness that seemed quite at variance with the earthy realism of much of their conversation on the subject of animals and sisters. If one met them in the street or on the country roads, they would greet one with equal courtesy, often removing their berets when doing so. If I were sketching, they would crowd up stealthily behind me and make whispered and wondrous comments to one another: '*c'est le moulin du Maître Le Tellier,*' '*chic, que c'est drôlement dessiné!*' I found such solemn politeness and such delicacy of language charming, as indicative of an elaborate *honnêteté française* pleasantly archaic, as well as providing a tribute to the patient work of a devoted corps of teachers, male and female, crusaders in the interest of *la laïcité* and republican rectitude. The little peasant boys and girls of this Perchois village spoke with the same serious gravity and application as those of Restif's childhood in Sacy, two hundred years earlier. Of course, both the Saving of *le Normandie* and my stays in the Orne were in 1935 and 1936; politeness and gravity in the presence of elders is not what one would associate with French children of the 1970s, though country ones might still retain the old formulae of greeting and respect.

At various times I have been an *assistant d'anglais* in three *lycées* of Paris and the Paris region: Saint-Louis, Michelet, and Hoche, taking conversation classes with the two pre-military *corniches*, Mangin and Leclerc, with *Navale* and 'X', in the first, and in a variety of classes in the other two. All three provided me with a not very tall *mirador* from which to observe *les moeurs scolaires*, the warring factions in the stone courtyards, the conspiratorial groups hanging about under the stone arcades or in dark corners, the fat, moustached Egyptian boys, the pampered sons of the Wafdist bourgeoisie, eating their way through breaks, and to get used to the initially terrifying roar of hundreds of voices, all shouting, punctuated at regular intervals by the piercing whistles of *les répètes*, as they attempted to marshal their hordes into lines, the insistent ringing of electric bells, and, in Saint-Louis, the sinister roll of a drum, as if to drown the voice of Louis XVI and to herald the heavy thud of the blade. Noise seems to have been written into the *lycée* system, as if to train its inmates for the barricades, sit-ins, Revolution, and *manif*. In the *restaurant des maîtres d'internat*, in all three *lycées*, the ceiling presented to the experienced eye, like a stellar chart, a culinary geography, upside-down, a map of France's vegetable wealth in reverse: long *flaques* of dark green representing spinach—the favourite missile—concentrations of small black dots like pellets, lentils (said, in Hoche, to have been derived from the gravel of the paths of the pious Maria Leszczinska's forecourt), the pale browns of *pois chiches*, other splashed colours less easy to identify, all witnessing to the contents of *trimestre* after *trimestre*, *année scolaire* on *année scolaire*, of plates hurled to the receptive ceiling, as the *maîtres* competed as to whose shot would stick longest, before falling down with a dull squelch, on the tables or on the floor, a few indeed remaining above our heads, sometimes for weeks on end, like green or brown stalactites. The *maîtres* took it out of the institutional food with the same inventive vigour as the *potaches* took it out of *them*. Eating in such athletic conditions was much more fun than being promoted to the staid frigidity reigning in the *restaurant des professeurs*. One could also do exchanges with nutritious pre-missiles that would give one, two, or three extra *quarts de vin*. It was an atmosphere to which one was quickly acclimatised.

At a much later stage, I taught for the Christian Brothers at the École des Francs-Bourgeois, near the church of Saint-Paul. They were a fierce, rough lot, the brothers, in their blue habits and white bands, with heavy, very red, pugilistic hands. The terrible, bearded Préfêt de Discipline spent the teaching hours moving round and round the cloisters, on to which all the class-rooms gave; a sudden pounce here: '*Dubois, debout, les bras en croix,*' and there: '*Esmenard, à genoux, au coin,*' each bellowed out in a voice that would have carried across the Champ de Mars, each accompanied by a massive clout that sent the recipient reeling, so that, often, when I came to take my class, half the boys would be kneeling with their faces to the wall, or standing, like storks, on one leg, their arms extended as on a cross (I might have thought the punishment had had some hidden religious symbolism, had not I witnessed similar treatment on the part of the well-named M. Bataille, an English teacher at Hoche and a well-known *laïc*, who regularly used up all the corners of his odd-shaped class-room with kneeling figures) on the sloping tops of their desks. Within minutes, a few more would be similarly incapacitated, on the massive Préfêt's next time round, so that many could not see the blackboard and most would not have a free hand with which to write. It was difficult enough to make myself heard in barrack-room English between the shouted sentences of the revolving disciplinarian. It was very much the same in the Pension Bigot, at Enghien-les-Bains, where, in addition, I first became aware of the delightful vagaries of French schoolboy and schoolgirl spelling, often only understandable when read to oneself aloud, a habit I had formed when confronted with documents and letters of the revolutionary period written by *sans-culotte* worthies or ultra-royalist bandits. It was interesting to try and guess the writer's provincial origin from his rendering of common words, provincial accents often clearly showing through such attempts on standard French. Parisian was easily recognisable under such brave disguises. *Chez Bigot*, the chaos was much the same as *chez les Frères*, the noise unbelievable, for there was no discipline at all. These *cancres* were all *paying* pupils, and their parents paid well.

So I soon acquired a rough-and-ready knowledge of the vocabulary of *lycée* and *pension*, most of it now out of date, as well as of the more endearing mis-spellings. And there is an intimacy about *les fautes d'orthographe* that is as unfailingly appealing in its mixture of naiveté, guile, and inventiveness, in the lined notebooks of school as in childishly written eighteenth-century letters to a *juge de paix*. I could feel myself as much at home with the anarchic reality of French children *en masse* as with the literary and evocative *roman scolaire*.

In the second half of the 1930s, my favourite authors in French were Maupassant and Courteline, Eugène Dabit and Panaït Istrati. What I most appreciated in Maupassant was his Norman topography, the reassuring geography of place-names ending in -ville, his awareness of the social hierarchies, and his exploitation of incidents in the Franco-Prussian War to develop a plot in a semiprivate situation. He was in so many ways the historian's ideal novelist. I could laugh, rather uneasily, with Courteline—uneasily, because, in the second half of the '30s, jokes about military service and *les grandeurs et les servitudes* could be distinctly disturbing to an Englishman in his late teens and early twenties. Courteline was a master at grotesque situations, and no writer has ever depicted with such skill the progressive stages of drunkenness; and I appreciated in Dabit and Istrati a sort of native innocence and wonder. Dabit's itineraries were familiar to me; Istrati's Braïla had the charm of exoticism. Both were fraternal and populist observers; Istrati's people were also picaresque. Later, during the War, I taught a young Polish airman, who came from the eastern borderland (Korzec, near Stanisławów) and who, having crossed into Rumania, was well treated by a group of Rumanian gipsies, who, passing him down the line, along their own secret itineraries, enabled him to live out what remained of his childhood in encampments on the edge of cities and deltas. By the time he reached England, via Syria and France, at a little over seventeen, he had seen a great deal and had enjoyed what he had seen. I encouraged him to write down, in such English as he could manage, an account of his Balkan wanderings, clad in sheepskin and rabbit, and of his early impressions of England. This he did, in a series of R.A.F. notebooks—a good use of government stationery—and in his own peculiar spelling. His account was subsequently published, in two numbers of *Life and Letters Today* of the summer of 1942. It is a work of no great literary merit; but it is written with engaging candour and presents a view of very public history from a level both private and childlike. Its intimacy cannot fail to appeal to the social historian. He later put his English to more practical use. But he was my best Polish pupil and I was quite proud to see his account in print.

Four of the authors included in this book I have known personally, Maxence van der Meersch, Louis Guilloux, and Jules Roy quite well, indeed as friends. Hervé Bazin I met in more formal conditions. Queneau, unfortunately, I never met. But none has been included on a basis so tenuous and so personal. I have little experience of literary circles, I am not a literary critic, and the authors with whom I am concerned are rarely outstanding. Some of them are little known, though I think they deserve to be better known; most have been forgotten. My rules of admission have not been literary skill, though, obviously, as one reads novels for pleasure rather than for historical information, one prefers a stylist like Françoise Sagan to a heavy-footed *piéton* like Zola, but historical and social insight. For instance, when recently reading, in Dijon, *Le Grand Dadais* (Poirot-Delpech) I was not only delighted by the glib style of his narrative, but also by his acute sensitivity to nuances of class in a Parisian context. There is a wonderful evocation of the hall—all that his hero saw of the place—of a house in the *noble faubourg*, the home of his aristocratic schoolmate at Janson de Sailly; and to have described the militant P.C.F. mother of another friend, living in les Batignolles, as having *la voix rauque* seemed to me a stroke of social genius; of course, I reminded myself, *all* my Communist friends had such voices, worn away no doubt by the repetitive shouting of boring slogans. In such proletarian circles, hoarseness could equal sincerity. The same friend's father sat down to dinner in a vest. The narrator, belonging to the middle ground, the dead father an officer in the Armée de l'Air, but an uncle an influential Senator and Académicien, takes it all in with avid fascination. I believe that all such novelists have in common too an awareness of place and period and a warm, if amused, concern for ordinary people—*les petites gens, les très petites gens*—living in the semi-privacy of shared itineraries, and that, with one or two notable exceptions, they all depict a confined and mapped world of reassuring banality. Unlike Céline, they are not haters, but rather indulgent, even affectionate, observers.

But perhaps I am imposing a coherence on what began in incoherence and accident, in a series of stages, and that then grew in self-indulgence and imagination, beyond novels written to novels as yet unwritten. The first stage was when I was elected to deliver the Zaharoff Lecture at Oxford, in February 1976 (it must be said for the then Vice-Chancellor, Sir John Habakkuk, that he could not have guessed what he had unwittingly set in motion). Having given my lecture on certain aspects of Queneau's novels, I decided to deliver sixteen lectures on the general theme of the French—and francophone—regional novel, a course aimed at those preparing for the Joint School of History and French, a combination which, though far from perfect, represents a very welcome new approach to the proper understanding of French society; but one in which History is the master, and language merely the parlour-maid, to appear when summoned by the bell. The third stage was when I repeated these lectures, some of them filled out with more explanatory material, as thirteen talks, given on B.B.C. Radio 3 (under the bizarre and unhelpful title of 'Fiction, Fact and France', a trinity not of my choice, but imposed from on high) on Sunday evenings, from April to September 1978. The present exploration closely follows the text of the talks; and I have not attempted to 'devocalise' what was often delivered on the spot without notes. This is a book that started life by being *talked*, often impromptu, over the table, to the kindly and reassuring presence of Michael Mason, my editor and producer and friend. Much of the section on the Thullier family was, however, omitted in the talks; and I have provided a new introduction to the two talks on Queneau, given on Radio 3, two years earlier, in 1976.

During my talks, each published (though most not in full) in the *Listener*, I derived both encouragement and information from the many listeners and readers who wrote to me with suggestions, criticisms, and requests for information. Thanks to them, I have been introduced to the sheer wonder of Marcel Pagnol's memories of childhood; an unpardonable omission in my talks that I have now remedied. Had it not been for the kindness and enthusiasm of my correspondents, I would not have been encouraged to produce my talks in the form of a book. As I received a great many letters, I cannot thank all my correspondents individually; but I hope that, in this amended and, I trust, improved, version, each will recognise his or her hand, in matters great and small. I would like also to thank the members of the Radio 3 Critics' Forum—a severe, august, and frightening panel—who, halfway through my talks—I had reached the peasant novel—showed both appreciation and some understanding (they did not fully understand that my approach was primarily that of a historian) about what I was attempting to evoke and pursue. They rightly insisted that my talks contained an element of self-indulgence; and self-indulgent they are, for they attempt to give expression to my visual and aural awareness of a country, a landscape, a people, and a language that I love and delight in, with, perhaps, the added benefit of nostalgia for something that is no longer quite what it was. But this is no doubt merely *la déformation de l'âge*; wonder and innocence belong more readily to the '30s than to the implacable '70s. They also, I think rightly, suggested that many of my allusions were obscure. I have tried to make them less so, especially by adding biographical notes on the authors mentioned.

The talks would never have been given, this book would never have been published, had it not been for the active help of two friends who, time and again, have kept me on course and have had the patience to locate repetition, vagueness, and contradiction. Michael Mason, as always the most inspired and inspiring of listeners, has provided me with a smiling audience of one. Richard Brain has, as on so many other occasions, seen me through, from original notion, to actual publication; and to him, once again, I owe the choice of a title that had persistently eluded me. Perhaps, too, I should thank novelists, both living and dead, who, over more than forty years, have given me so much pleasure and joy, so many insights into history, so many hints to the exercise of historical imagination, and such a sense of intimacy and reassurance.

Wolvercote, 25 February 1979

. . . Me promenant un soir sur le pont,[1] je fus salué d'un air de prétention par une jolie pécheresse. . . . *Vous êtes étranger, car je ne vous connais pas—Un français ne l'est point dans le royaume, vous voulez dire que je ne suis pas normand—C'est cela—.* . . . Nous voilà en route . . . une petite porte d'une petite maison se présenta; un escalier obscur et sinueux où je fus conduit par la main, me fit arriver à une chambre assez propre, où je trouvai une seconde nymphe aussi maniérée; c'était la soeur de ma conductrice. . . . l'une étoit brune, l'autre blonde, et toutes deux affligées de 17 à 18 ans. . . . J'offris de manger une poularde. . . .

Les Amours de Cartouche, à Paris, de l'imprimerie Forget, an VI (1797-8)

[1] Le Grand Pont, Rouen

PART ONE

1

The Threshold

The historian of *les petites gens* and the novelist of urban or regional populism, though they are concerned with different but still closely related disciplines, have one thing, one overriding need in common—the ability to see, a sense of place that is concrete, almost physical, even if it is addressing itself to a town or a quarter or a landscape of nearly two centuries back. Such visual awareness must take in the most minute details of domestic architecture—the colour and shape of shutters, the position and size of doors and windows, the tiny hints afforded by a staircase off a dark court-yard, as it curls upwards, the tempting threshold between what is public and visible and what is private, yet suggestible.

A patient and repetitive enumeration of detail, including the contents of pockets, how clothes are laid out on the chair at night, how many people sleep to a room, at what times of the day people may sit out on the street, or on the front steps of their houses, to enjoy the spring sunshine or the evening cool, to observe the street and those who pass in it, those who live opposite, the comings and goings at upper windows, where people who don't know one another by name and are anxious to know one another by name are most likely to meet, without calling attention to themselves from others; why churches offer such excellent, because unobtrusive, unobserved meeting-places; what people might do with their spare time, what are their likeliest itineraries within a quarter or a town; what they will wear when anxious to impress or to please . . . all these things will enable the historian to reach beyond artificial collectivities (because I think most collectivities are textbook creations imposed upon quite unknowing groups a century or more later), down to the level of the individual or the family, or of friends or workmates, surprised in the privacy of personal hopes and fears, reasonable expectations, and humble enjoyments, giving to his work the conviction of close observation, *la chose vue*, and of conversation not meant to be heard, yet overheard.

In this respect, the task of the historian may be rather more difficult than that facing the novelist, because the novelist is better situated—in time, if not in place: the novelist will often have actually observed the tiny pieces of material evidence—for instance, the government 'Utility' mark on an article of clothing to indicate the early or middle 1940s, as observed, for instance, with her usual accuracy, by the novelist Beryl Bainbridge, writing about the suburbs of Liverpool, the Fylde peninsula, in the 1940s.

In order to carry conviction, the historian must be equally alert to such minutiae—to the texture of stone, the coldness of metal, the rough feeling of fustian, the softness of corduroy, the sheen of silk, the colour of wool, the cadence and local accent behind reported speech, the movement of a body in repose, or in sudden agitation, the manner of walking, indicative of the manner of earning, or of a whole attitude to life in general, the ambience of the day, of the week, of the season; the sound of rain.

Such attention to detail isn't designed only to carry conviction, but also to produce enjoyment, which is as much the function of history, as it is that of a romance. Both the novelist and the historian are writing about individuals, lonely ones or gregarious ones, seeking company or avoiding it, but—at least, for instance, in eighteenth-century urban conditions—finding it almost impossible to avoid, conditioned by their immediate physical environment. Both must be concerned with what would matter most to such individuals, each seen as unique, a person precious in his or her own right.

Each must then understand the immediate, immense importance of personal honour to an eighteenth-century shop assistant, a serving-girl, the daughter of an artisan; honour will mark her place in a close, cruelly observant, and very hierarchical neighbourhood.

Each must perceive the perilous balance between fear and courage on which an artisan or a proud soldier must proceed in order to maintain the respect of a demanding entourage, and yet preserve himself from unnecessary physical danger—and so allowance must also be made for permissible and non-permissible cowardice. Attention to such detail is archivally—materially therefore—possible for the historian who knows where to look for his material.

The novelist, of course, has managed to create it, out of a fund of close observation, because no individual can be totally indifferent: no one can be stripped down simply to the uniformity of institutional clothing, the clothing of a dragoon or a hussar. It is also a matter of attempted accuracy—necessarily, of course, a pretty large jump into the unknown: 'He must have', 'she would have', 'it must have seemed'—and so on and so forth. An impressionistic use of the conditional, much encountered in these talks, is entirely excusable, I think, if based on long acclimatisation, visual and oral experience and alertness, long familiarity with a variety of archival material, and a sympathetic susceptibility to the innumerable nuances of local ambience.

The historian labours under the disadvantage (if, as I do, he works on a popular level in the eighteenth or early nineteenth centuries) of not being able to hear his subjects, having to rely on documents—official or institutional, both generally written by others—so that he has to take on the further mental effort of translating them back into what must have been direct speech, a process that some recent French historians have described, perhaps somewhat grandly, as *l'oralisation de l'histoire*—a flattering description indeed of the speech of those recorded by such an observer as Restif de la Bretonne, those who massacre French grammar in the manner of *'j'avons'* and who pepper sentences with military and nautical expletives: *'millepipes'*, *'milles-ieus'*, *'franc comme l'ail '*, and so on. The novelist, on the other hand, can accumulate such material, both visual and oral, from direct observation.

However, cities, towns, quarters, villages, don't change overnight; a great deal of the concrete evidence needed by the historian will still be on the ground today, even if it has been cleaned up often beyond recognition, even if a once busy and living street has been converted into the deadliness of a pedestrian precinct. If he is prepared to abandon the show-places—the *voies triomphales*, the successive pomposities of state architecture, the wide boulevards that statue-fy collective conformity in the frozen orthodoxy of official unanimity—to seek out the courtyards and workshops, the alleyways and closed passages, the semi-private, semi-secret *cités* or *villas* with iron gates to close them in at night, he must go about his search on foot, walking along abandoned railway lines, or little-used canals, behind breakers' yards and small chaotic workshops, and industrial waste, the borderlands of cities, the gasworks, the cemeteries, the marshalling yards, and bus depots, and bus cemeteries, two-decker trams converted into houses and covered in greenery.

An apparently abandoned cottage may be just visible between thick tentacular creeper, still indicating life, and a jealously guarded, fierce privacy, with seven padlocks on the door, and many threatening notices, '*chien méchant*', and the evidence of love and care in a tiny garden decorated with scallop-shells arranged in rings stuck in earth filling old petrol cans nestling against the high wire netting—*la maison du sauvage*, a small temple of individualism, an artisanal folly, by a Sunday architect.

Having had to spend days, or weeks, in many small French provincial towns and villages, preparing material for my book *Les Armées révolutionnaires*, I have experienced again and again the excitement and the reassurance of gradually discovering the ambience of a locality, its pattern of movement through the day, by an itinerary, fixed in advance by a hotel at one end, and by the *dépôt d'archives* at the other—a purely arbitrary geography, that may often miss out the showpieces, but that may also compensate with unexpected treasures on the way. The result has also been that I tend to relate a novel to the place in which I acquired it and read it.

One should, I think, read French novels in France, and English ones in England, and both while thus on the move. For they then acquire new and unexpected dimensions. I dare say it is also a matter of age; quite recently, I re-read *Crime and Punishment*, something that I read first when I was eighteen, and on re-reading it I discovered in it the really immense and permanent presence of the topography of St. Petersburg, its many islands, its estuaries, its rivers and inlets, its swing-bridges, its long, long stretches of iron railings, and the bustle and filth of the quarter known as the Hay Market: a novel, in fact, about people in a town—and this was something that I had totally missed the first time that I read it. I like to reassure myself with the thought that, given time and patience and the freedom to pry into courtyards and to push behind the public streets and public buildings, something of that anarchical and individualistic city may still be found surviving, in hidden places, in the place that is now called Leningrad.

Having been subjected for four or five years to the obligation of wearing a uniform, I am also very much aware of the importance of clothing as a form of self-assertion, and also as a reassurance of individual identity. When I was in Roubaix I was given an old brown jacket by Monsieur Roussel—Alphonse—an enormous man, so that when I wore it, while working at night, it hung on me. It also had a thin red ribbon, in the lapel, a red ribbon that gave me a certain amount of satisfaction. When I put this jacket on I felt that I had, as it were, removed myself from a military collectivity. Later, at different times, I was given the discarded clothing of Italian and French friends, wearing each in turn with a sense of enrichment, as if I were extending my identity; going about in the clothes of others I was somehow getting closer to the lives of others. Perhaps this is rather a romantic view of objects. But objects, like itineraries, are reassuring, because they are claims on an uncertain future, and they appear to be guarantees of continuity. It is the ultimate reassurance of the continuity of individualism and of human variety, that we seek both in local literature and in local popular history.

During my time in the army as a very unwilling soldier, I held on, whenever I could, to two forms of escape. One was the possession of a snuffbox in the shape of a ram's horn with a silver-hinge top, enclosing a red stone—given to me by my sister. That followed me from posting to posting, until its disappearance and its replacement, while on leave in Toulouse, by a small eighteenth-century jug of Martres-Tolosane ware, both being reminders of another world, private and civilian.

The other form of escape was when I was still in England. In each locality of posting, there was a front room, to which I could go in the evening to enjoy the immense luxury of being alone, and to read, with the door closed and with a view through potted plants and lace curtains onto a street reassuring in its endlessly reproducible banality, and yet also a street of safety, privacy, and modest expectations.

In France, in Belgium, and in Germany, I had to make do with whatever came my way. But there was always somewhere, the class-room and the vegetable garden, of the École Communale in Barbeville outside Bayeux, the house of the novelist Maxence van der Meersch in Wasquehal by the Canal de Roubaix, the cellar of the Diedericx family in the rue du Couloir in Ixelles, a whitewashed, black-beamed low cottage in Iserlohn belonging to the family of a large blonde girl called Dorothea. . . .

The sort of history that I enjoy, and that I try to write, is about private people and private places; about obscure people in public places. It is a form of reassurance and enrichment, because it is utterly varied and because (to misquote the haunting words of Ramuz's *Histoire du Soldat*) 'ce qui a été, sera.'

And so I find the same form of enjoyment, enrichment, and reassurance in the novel that is firmly set in time and place and privacy as I do in my own sort of history. Indeed, I cannot see very much difference between these two forms of observation and entertainment, experience and compassion.

2

Childhood

In literary memory, the most retentive and perceptive period is nearly always that of *childhood*, or, at least, of childhood and adolescence recalled and reconstructed, perhaps not without arts, embellishment, and invention, at a much later date, from the more selective platform of adult observation. In the eyes of childhood—eyes that are generally not nearly as candid as they look —colours are brighter, yellows are yellower, scarlet is ruddier, the light, fast-changing skies of the Île-de-France or of the Bourbonnais, happier, fuller of promise and of scurrying movement—with the imminence of a sudden shower of rain—the brooding Vlaminck skies of French Flanders and the Pas-de-Calais, dwarfing the low white red-roofed farmhouses, the long lines of back-to-backs in dirty brick, broken only by the different frontage of an *estaminet*: Motte-Cordonnier, of a shop: les Docks du Nord, huddling themselves as if to seek protection in the jostling of brick and plaster from a vast horizon torn by the north-easterly gales, fuller of menace, sadness, snow, and war, but also announcing presents, the fire-crackers and the snow fights of the Saint-Nicolas. In the Midi, all is stillness, heat, and silence, broken only by the persistent calls of the *cigales*, and perhaps by the sound, shrill and carrying far, of a small girl, reading out loud from a reading-book, with her strangely open vowels echoing across a brilliantly white *cour de ferme*.

The sun is brighter, the summers are longer, though even more implacably threatened by the steady approach of *la Rentrée*, the interruption of holiday friendships and the beginning or fulfilment of adolescent love, despite so many protests, as claims on the future and pathetic attempts to prolong the wonder of holidays far into the autumnal grind of *lycée* and convent.[1] '*On se reverra*', '*Paris*

---

[1] '. . . Je tentai donc de supprimer le mois d'octobre. Il se trouvait dans l'avenir, et offrait donc moins de résistance qu'un fait du présent. . . .' When all attempts to keep dread October at arm's length had failed and the *Rentrée* had taken place, then the child Marcel Pagnol would attempt to cling to some material object—in this case a trap laid for birds or small animals and used during the summer months in the aromatic hills overlooking Marseilles—that still offered a physical link to a lost rural

n'est pas le bout du monde', and so on; but one won't, once the persistent iodine smell of seaweed has receded, overcome by that of the
Métro, once the bruises and scratches caused by climbing over the
rocks, in search of sea anemones, are healed and covered by thick,
sensible winter socks and stockings.

Such sensitivity to the full range of the seasons, their colours,
their smells, to warmth, damp, and cold, is much more acute,
perhaps even at the time, and certainly in cherished retrospect, than
when dulled by the daily routine of employment and the regular urban itineraries of a respectable occupation. Listen, for instance, to
Grenadou, a seventy-five-year-old peasant from the cornfields of
the Beauce, as he was taped by a journalist, Alain Prévost, who
made a book out of his recorded recollections, listen to this old man
evoking the summers of the Beauce before 1914, before that particular day in August when he and his companions were called in
from the fields by the persistent clanging tocsin, an awful sort of
herald of doom, from the village church, so that they went into the
village to read the big notice headed by crossed flags, in that thick
and rather archaic type favoured by French officialdom:
'*République Française—Mobilisation Générale*'—and then all of
them, perhaps a dozen or so young men, walking to Chartres, to be
fitted up with the sky-blue uniforms. Grenadou will still argue that
those summers were endlessly bright, that the vast cornfields of the
Beauce were yellower, that the corn itself was taller, than at any
time since 1918.

Listen, too, to Colette, in so many of her novels, retaining, even
in her marvellously placed flat overlooking the arcades of the
Palais-Royal, retaining well on into old age, her face that of a
rather battered pierrot, still giving off an air of astonished innocence and surprise, the pointed vowels and rolling Rs of an *accent du terroir*, somewhere in Burgundy, evoking her country
childhood, and there again the bees are so much fatter, their buzz
so much more insistent, the fruit is lusher and the figs are greener,
then mauver and more succulent, and the white dresses are whiter,
the blue smocks bluer, the yellow straw hats yellower, and the
glowing coals of dark eyes darker, as though, with each year of
progressing age, the colours had lost a little more of their bright-
ness, and become diluted, paler, and more tired.

paradise of freedom and sun: '. . . Ma main, dans ma poche, serrait un piège, qui
n'avait plus sa valeur meurtrière, mais qui devenait un objet sacré, une relique, une
promesse. . . .' Marcel Pagnol, *Le Château de ma mère*.

Listen, too, to Valéry Larbaud, in his numerous reminiscences, and more especially in his evocative *Enfantines*—Valéry Larbaud, a permanent invalid, paralysed from the waist downwards, recalling the marvellous summers of a very well-to-do childhood near Vichy. (His mother was one of the owners of one of the principal *sources*—Vichy Célestins.) Recalling a childhood in this beautiful part of France, the Bourbonnais, when he could still run about and explore, climb trees, hide with his sister, and with the very carefully selected children of neighbours who met with his mother's approval. The garden seems quite limitless, almost as extensive as a continent—its high stone walls, covered in pears and figs, seem like frontiers between states. And how many frontiers this Vichy-born child had already crossed in the blue and gold luxury, the creaking rosewood, and magnificent brass fittings of the Compagnie Internationale des Wagons-Lits des Grands Express Européens, the very epitome of solid Belgian luxury, by the age of twelve, when he had already travelled to Madrid, St. Petersburg, England, Berlin, Italy, and so on.

Here is the child, in sailor suit and wide straw hat, fitted with an elastic band around his neck, here he is, striding through the waist-high pampas grass and ferns in his grandmother's garden, in the Allier, a lush, green paradise. He is le Capitaine Brazza of the French marines. Here is Valéry Larbaud in this role opening up the *brousse*, the thick jungle; he is an intrepid officer in the *fusiliers-marins* himself, exploring the upper reaches of the Congo, its wide waters darkened by overhanging trees and coils of suppurating plants. And listen again to Valéry Larbaud in adolescent discovery of the exotic, handsome, immensely rich sons and daughters of South American millionaires, in a private school, on the heights of Saint-Cloud, overlooking Paris: *Fermina Marquez*, the most formed of his novels.

Listen, also, to the young Pascal Jardin, whose father was secretary to Pierre Laval during the occupation years, as, with considerable malice, very acute nine-year-old observation, and rather delicious humour, from a very much battered and very much married mid-thirties, he recalls acting a play with his sister in the presence of the very *fine fleur* of collaboration in his father's house near Vichy: Abetz, Laval, the lugubrious, sad, yellow-faced Georges Bonnet, the Papal Nuncio, always clothed by Jeanne Lanvin, who used to make his beautiful silk soutanes, the Minister of Education, wearing make-up, his eyes running with henna in the heat, the Spanish Ambassador to Vichy France, decked out like a sort of Philip II galleon, and covered in braid and medals, so that he can hardly sit down. And listen to him again, later, evoking his truly wretched schooldays back in France, after having been privately educated for a time in Switzerland, where his father took refuge, at the Lycée d'Évreux, followed by remarks to his back: '*Il est fils de collabo.*'

Best of all, of course, the evocation of the sheer wonder of childhood, mystery and escape, a landscape of mists and damp parks, of reeded lakes glowing as if floating in the lowering sky, a flat-bottomed green boat, moored invitingly to a rotting landing-place, long avenues of ancient trees, rusty gates, permanently chained up and surmounted by complicated heraldic devices held up by marine monsters, the grass growing high in the once-tended carriageway—best of all, I suppose, that wonderful evocation, *le monde féerique* of *Le Grand Meaulnes*, Alain-Fournier's single novel, situated on the borders of the Cher and the Indre in that part of France just south of the Loire which was also the home of George Sand—an area with placenames also full of a similar limpidity, of muted colour, small market-towns with names like Blanc, Argent. The moorlands and parklands of what has so often been called, and so wrongly called, *la triste Sologne*, to which the adolescent imagination of Alain-Fournier gave this quality of pervasive magic and innocence, wonder, and mystery. And revisited perhaps by a reader, what is it then?—just an old, ill-kempt park, the trees rotting, stagnant ponds, not lakes at all, and the once grand entrance to a lost château, a lot of old iron hanging rustily on a couple of hinges, giant ferns and fungi, growing almost body-high, an invasive smell of damp, rot, and decomposition, overgrown paths, abandoned riding-tracks, *clairières* choked with pink weed, an overtipped urn, a rather melancholy sphinx still on its pedestal, its twin paws neatly aligned on the top, therefore a *good* sphinx, staring blindly down a long vista leading nowhere. One feels, perhaps, that it was just as well that Alain-Fournier never returned to an area degraded, emptied of mystery, several thicknesses of rotting leaves.

In the memory of that strange man Henri Béraud, already a member of the Fat Club, the *Club des cent kilos*, already a regular visitor to the Munich beer feast, and, indeed, a very respectable contestant for the European championship of the fattest man in Europe, already accepted also as a personality *sur la place de Paris*, as a journalist, and as a novelist, and as a polemicist, listen to him, in his novel, *La Gerbe d'or*, evoking a distant childhood spent in the Quartier des Terreaux in central Lyons—a world of entirely reassuring proportions, safe rules, the closed code of a local vocabulary, as he plays with his classmates, *les gones de Lyon*, and the terribly dangerous and fast-moving and green Rhône. The extraordinarily up-and-down town, remembered from Paris, seems even more up-and-down than ever in *La Gerbe d'or*—the Montée de la Grande Côte, which, I suppose, is one of the steepest streets of any city in Europe, and even the pedestrian can only walk up it by holding on to the iron chains that are provided for that purpose, as it climbs up to the old silk suburb of La Croix Rousse—La Montée de la Grande Côte, as steep as the dangerous zigzag green and yellow climb to heaven, each zigzag patrolled by some terrible apocalyptic beast, breathing fire, in one of those late nineteenth-century popular prints. And at the top, that great stone, Le Gros Caillou, a small meteorite placed on the very top of La Croix Rousse. Or that other hill, equally dramatic, the green slopes of Fourvière, known to the Lyonnais as *la colline noire*, as the clerical hill, on the top a pseudo-Eiffel Tower and the basilica and the archiepiscopal palace of the Primate of the Gauls, rather like the slopes of the imaginary island which is thickly clothed in greenish-blue vegetation in one of those landscapes, extraordinarily up-and-down landscapes of Bosch or the elder Brueghel. In Béraud's memory, the buses and the old horse-trams had never been so red; Bellecour, the huge, prestigious square in central Lyons between the two rivers, La Place Bellecour, never so vast, or the town itself, seen from the heights of the Croix Rousse, so blue. There is a marvellous passage in *La Gerbe d'or*, as Béraud looks over his city on an autumn day, one of the very rare clear days when the mists are not rising from the two rivers, and he looks over central Lyons right to its tip where the two rivers meet at Perrache and Ainay, and the seabirds are wheeling over the city, and he evokes *la ville bleue, ma ville*, the steep houses so black . . . rather sinister, the ceilings tall enough to accommodate a full *métier* for a silk worker. The birds circling over the two rivers, so numerous and so strident, and the fearful and wild Rhône so very green. Even though he spent an adult life dragging his more than *cent kilos* across the whole of Europe as a journalist and a star reporter for *Le Matin*, *Le Journal*, *Le Petit Parisien*, Berlin, Moscow, Munich, Béraud, a sad figure in post-liberation France, condemned to death for collaboration, finally pardoned by the President of the Republic, Béraud, retaining his father's bulk, continues to speak in the slow, lazy, rather diffident, accent of Lyons: '*Alors, M. Cobb, vous revoilà de nouveau à Lyon, vous vous plaisez à Lyon*'—as he recalls the children, his companions, *les gones de Lyon,* with whom he had played underneath the Pont de la Guillotière on the wide, cobbled quays of the Rhône, Béraud, in the innocence of his evocation of a childhood in Lyons spent in his father's shop, building up strength on his father's celebrated *pâtisseries* and cream cakes, for it was not for nothing that Béraud *père* was the President of L'Association Professionnelle des Mâitres Boulangers-Pâtissiers du Département du Rhône.

Hervé Bazin, a novelist from a very different part of France, from the West, in his first novel, *Vipère au poing*, a novelist to whom sheer hate, undiluted hate, has lent the vengeful, wide, dark wings of a marvellously powerful literary style, what one could, indeed, call *une prose vengeresse* if ever there was one, as he recalls his detested mother, Folcoche, 'Folcochon', encased in black, his wretched, hopeless father, a parody of the clerical and very academic—I mean academic in the sense of Académie Française—uncle René Bazin—perhaps his best-known book is *Les Oberlé*—recreates the wet seawinds and the damp of a very, very dilapidated manor house in the Craonnais—a lake again, a lake in the garden, almost choked with reeds, another green, rotting boat half filled with water and dead leaves, but yet still afloat and so at least manoeuvrable by Hervé and by his brother, Frédéric; in a successful attempt to tip the detested mother in, the two boys beating her over the head with their oars, Hervé encouraging his younger brother—'*Vas-y, Freddie, tape bien fort!*'—as, her black weeds billowing out like a crinoline, and her yellow face rising and lowering in the thick greenish scum, swimming like a dog, she heads strongly for the shore, from which she mocks the efforts of her two legitimate sons—himself, Hervé, his brother Freddie, and his half-brother, a love-child of Folcoche's, constantly sneezing with colds. The two boys (not the love-child, though) sleep in back numbers of *La Croix* and *Ouest-Eclair*, two papers that suit both the rather clerical family and the part of France they live in, sleeping in newspapers in lieu of sheets. It is always damp, it is nearly always raining, and the actual extent of the damp can be measured at mealtimes by the extending or receding *carte de France* formed on the mouldy beige-coloured tapestry, a tapestry depicting the surrender of Pocahontas, an eighteenth-century Gobelins tapestry, that covers the west wall of the salon of this damp *manoir*. It is true also that there are brief interludes of summer sunshine, when the pretty Craonnaises have their skirts billowing up to reveal strong and stocky legs—*basses sur pattes*, as in the flat Vendée, under a teasing westerly gale.

In Raymond Queneau's *Un Rude Hiver*—again an evocation of his own childhood as the son of a haberdasher in the most fashionable street in Le Havre, naturally called the rue de Paris—he recalls the bitter, cold, and windy winter of 1916 to 1917, at a time when, if the wind was in the right direction, the child could hear (or could imagine that he heard) the guns of the Western Front. In this book, the wind, too, is always blowing gale force as the child struggles along the promenade, the Boulevard Maritime; it is always winter and the sea is always rough, there are always white horses as far out as one can see, and the children from the working-class port area, Quai de Nouméa, roam the town in thirteen- and fourteen-year-old packs. They are always drunk, they are always smoking cigarettes, cigarettes that they have obtained, Woodbines and so on, from the British base. Their fathers are away at the war, their mothers are either engaged in war work, or possibly they are patriotically entertaining the Allied officers, British, New Zealand, Australian, and Canadian—and, indeed, the Belgians; these are there, as it were, for ever, walking either up and down the Boulevard Maritime or up and down the Boulevard de Strasbourg or up and down the central rue de Paris. The passage of time in this novel is marked at regular intervals by the insistent timbre of the bell each time the door of his mother's shop is opened. And what an excellent position from which to witness a town and childhood, that of a shop—like Béraud.

Another wartime childhood recalled above all the truly astonishing figure, the extraordinarily eccentric figure of Cripure, who is a *professeur de littérature* or *professeur de lettres* in the *lycée*—and, of course, children are particularly acute witnesses to the almost endless eccentricities and extravagant appearances of their different schoolmasters—*Prof de Lycée*, *surgé* in schoolboy language, for *surveillant général, répète*, that proletarian of French education, *le répétiteur*. All this is firmly placed, Cripure above all, in the implacably inbred, very clerical, and very patriotic cathedral town of Saint-Brieuc in Brittany, a past from which, even now, safe in Paris and employed in the publishing house of Gallimard, Louis

Guilloux is unable still to escape, this memory of the First World War in his native town of Saint-Brieuc. Marvellously evoked, particularly thanks to the figure of Cripure and his mistress and his various domestic animals and pets, in his vast and meandering and chaotic novel of childhood, *Le Sang noir*. Salt, wind, ozone, the smell of fish, again rain, *la bruine*, that particularly fine rain of the Breton peninsula. Scudding clouds riding in low from the sea, a geography almost as despairing as the piteous wails of the seagulls.

In the very apocalyptic, endlessly and rather fussily moralising Demo-Christian prospect offered by the French novelist of Belgian origin (his family originally came from Flemish-speaking Bruges) Maxence van der Meersch (and what a typically northern Christian name to have), an implacably urban geography—brick, woollen mills, tram-lines, *estaminets*, canals, locks, and the dark and rather oily cobbles of the north, the terrible *pavé du nord* which is the terror of Belgian, Dutch, and French professional cyclists as they tackle the most frightful of all the long-distance cycle-races, Paris to Roubaix—is exploited really only as a constant background to the blind and brutal Saturday-night, week-end violence of alcoholism and of gin-drinking.

His Lille/Roubaix—Tourcoing—the twin wool towns, spilling over at twenty or thirty frontier posts into the kingdom of Belgium—reeks permanently of *le genef*, *genièvre* (a type of gin), and, less threatening, of the rich and very varied aromas that come across that frontier: cigarettes, tobacco, cheroots, and chocolate—Aros jaunes, Saint-Michel, Bastos, *nérons* (small cheroots), *bolivars* (for some peculiar reason, large cheroots). Maxence van der Meersch grew up in Roubaix—Tourcoing under the first German occupation, and was seven when, coming home from school one day, he saw the Prussian cavalry clattering through La Grand' Place—uhlans.

In his novel about the first German occupation of Roubaix—Tourcoing and Lille, which is called, appropriately, *Invasion Quatorze*, the German soldiers are not at all the sort of semi-mythical bogey figures in spiked helmets that one would encounter in illustrated children's books like those of the Alsatian, Hansi, who was a great propagator of anti-German feeling after 1870. Not at all, they were just rather poor, frightened, and really quite cunning fellows engaged, after 1916 and 1917, in complicated transactions on the black market, which was inevitably flourishing in this frontier area, and often had Roubaisienne girl-friends. In the autumn of 1918, Maxence, then an observant eleven, notices without much surprise, indeed with some relief—because they have really become quite part of the daily landscape familiar to him, and because they have shared in the same terrible hardships, and because they have been reduced to the same pitiful rations, *occupant* and *occupé* are looking very much the same; and they had very much the same preoccupations—he notices, after the departure of the German army in some confusion (the officers pulling off their epaulettes and this sort of thing; there is an air of revolution about the apparent break-up of the marvellous discipline of the German army), some of these familiar faces, after prudent disappearance for a week or two, all at once re-emerge from the green doors of the slum quarters, of the *corons*—the back-to-backs—in civilian clothes that rather tend to hang on them.

It is still a very vast geography, as recalled in *Invasion Quatorze*, one as pulled out, as long, as the truly apparently endless rue aux Longues Haies, the longest street in Roubaix, the one that leads slowly up to the Belgian frontier. As so often in industrial towns, its name is a sort of derision of the sad facts of industrial architecture, because there are no hedges here at all and no green whatever anywhere in the town; indeed, there is very little in the town other than brick and *pavé*. Light-green trams clatter upwards towards Lannoy, Lys-lèz-Lannoy, and the Belgian frontier—a sort of beyond, an *outre*-Mouscron, which was still very much part of the child's perception of work, leisure, and movement. Members of his family indeed, his uncles, his mother's brothers, supplement their fairly meagre incomes making uniforms for the German army in the textile mills, with tobacco smuggling, while the *frontaliers*, mostly Flemish-speaking, pour into the town to work, either in the mills or on the roads. Thus the frontier to the young Maxence is not at all a frontier in the way it would be to most people, and he can see very little difference between the republic and the kingdom—and how would he, when single houses or single cafés, or single *cafés-tabacs*, are actually divided, and if you walk from one end of the room or one end of the bar to another you are walking from the republic of France into the kingdom of Belgium?

Not very far to the east of van der Meersch's confined and urban world, Félicien Marceau, who is now an exile living in Paris, in *Bergère légère*, can still recall from the exile of Paris the cigar smell, and the smell, also, of fried potatoes, and those wide avenues of rather ugly, forbidding, red houses, described by Belgians as *style Léopold II*—a style heavy, grandiose, and extremely pretentious, as perhaps suited to the long-reigning millionaire king and owner of his own private colony of the Congo, which he left in his will to his kingdom. He recalls those suburbs of Brussels: Anderlecht, Etterbeek, Saint-Josse-ten-Noode, Saint-Gilles, Forest, Uccle, Woluwé-Saint-Pierre, Auderghem—and the cream-coloured tram-cars (many, alas, recently suppressed as a result of the construction of the Brussels Métro) of *le grand Bruxelles*, Greater Brussels.

Most vivid of all is the memory of an interior in a very quiet street, a very discreet street, just off the busy Porte de Namur in the upper city. There are pink lampshades; in fact, a predominant, gently diffused pink—pink curtains with pompoms, even the photographs encased in embroidered pink mounts, an embroidered firescreen depicting a bespectacled *roi soldat*, *Roi Albert*, Albert of the Belgians of First World War fame. There is an abundance of pouffes, a divan occupied by a line of hideously embroidered dolls dressed as pierrots, and six—no less—effigies of the Manneken-Pis in six different costumes, one of them as a Highlander, another as a Grenadier Guardsman, another dressed up as an officer in the Belgian National Guard of the last century, brightly coloured, in cheap porcelain, crowding the tops of consoles lined with mother-of-pearl. There is a constant aroma of coffee plus chicory (no self-respecting Bruxelloise would ever make coffee without chicory) and there are big, polished brass pots with rather sad green plants, bronze gladiators and bronze horses fighting for the possession of a heavy black clock on a crowded mantelpiece, corner cupboards stacked with ceramic souvenirs and miniature chamber-pots bearing suitably vulgar messages from La Panne, La Zoute—*le lit-toral belge*—Ostend, or from the interior—Binche, Dinant, Malines, Anvers, Damme. An interior that could certainly be described as comfortable, as *douillet*, and, indeed, of the same sort of almost overpoweringly respectable banality as the ground-floor rooms of neighbouring *tavernes*, as glimpsed from the quiet street and giving absolutely no hint of the activities of the pink-frocked lady when she moves down a storey. An extraordinarily eloquent evocation of one of the most oppressively and yet reassuringly middle-class cities in the world, in which the tram-drivers wear long-peaked caps and the *contrôleuses* military-styled *bonnets de police* with pompoms hanging rather like large acorns at the level of the tip of a pretty snub nose. A childhood marked out by magnificent and succulent *pâtisseries*—with regiments of chocolate-and-cream *têtes-de-nègre* to tempt the inhabitant of the *athénées royaux* (Belgium does not have *lycées*: it has those delightfully named schools, *athénées*, and they are not national, but *athénées royaux*) on his or her way home.

A language, too, of remarkable savour and rich coarseness, the sight and sound of brass bands and extravagant uniforms; even the railwaymen have a brass band with extravagant uniforms, making them look as though they were all admirals in the Belgian navy; Ensor country—that curious Anglo-Belgian painter who lived and died in Ostend. There are the sweet and rather pungent smell of the lethal fermented beer, la Gueuse Lambic, and, of course, the extraordinary linguistic bizarreries of the slum quarter, Quartier des Marolles, in the shadow of the dreadful Palais de Justice, which you might say is not just *style Léopold II*, but super-*style Léopold II*, itself a sort of vast piece of pastry, a huge *pièce montée*, perhaps the most frightful building anywhere in nineteenth-century Europe, origin of the most frightful insult that exists in Belgian French and which is always very closely followed by blows, the smashing of chairs, the smashing of glass, and so on: '*espèce d'architecte!*'

And what an extraordinary language it is! Neither French nor Flemish, a bit of both and producing such deliciously savorous phrases as '*espèce de tonnenklinker*' (for somebody who spends his time getting beer out of the barrels carried by horse-drawn drays—you put a sharply pointed knife in and you get a marvellous spout of beer coming out, for which you would be suitably provided with buckets and so on—that is a *tonnenklinker*). Or somebody who merely has curly hair is an '*espèce de krollerkop*'. Yet a terrain rich in provincialism as particularist as that of Liège, and almost entirely denied literary evocation, outside the work of Félicien Marceau, save, of course, in the particular case of Liège, by Georges Simenon, in his numerous accounts of his own childhood in the Quartier d'Outremeuse, where his mother died in her nineties only a few years ago, and his early days as a cub reporter on the local newspaper, *La Meuse*, before he, like so many other Belgian writers, moved off to Paris. He was aged barely twenty.

I have spoken so far of central France, western France, the Franco-Belgian frontier, and Brussels. Have, then, the southerners, the Méridionaux, no memory of childhood? There is indeed little enough to go on, though, for Marseilles and its wild aromatic hinterland, the enchanted hills and valleys of the *garrigue* and the

pinèdes, and the wonderful freedom offered by the bluish rocks and
the lime-greens of wild vineyards, we can return, again and again,
with delight, to the apparent innocence, disguising both skill and
guile, a very retentive memory and a very observant eye, of Marcel
Pagnol's four volumes of childhood memoirs: *La Gloire de mon
père*, *Le Château de ma mère*, *Le Temps des secrets*, and *Le Temps
des amours*. Each carries with it the scent of wild herbs growing
among reddish rocks, the very ancient odours of classical Greece,
the acute, almost tactile sensitivity to colour and texture—the
washed-out blue of a peasant's hand-cart, the brilliant yellow and
green of a darting lizard, the sharp red of a tiled roof, the peeling
bark of plane-trees, the dark, bluish green of a small pine, bending
in the direction of the prevailing mistral, the author's sense sharp-
ened by nostalgia for the lost paradise of a childhood spent hunting in the tawny hills and following secret itineraries revealed to
him by his little peasant friend, a boy too of twelve, Lili. But Pagnol
combines this visual sense with an awareness of period, the stable
provincial world of before 1914, when the *palmes académiques*
could still crown a career of educational devotedness, when
amateur poets wore floppy black hats and *lavallières*, when a
proviseur and even a *censeur* were distant, even mysterious figures,
of tremendous eminence, envied, feared, quoted, viewed from afar,
the living embodiments of the unbelievable summit of a career and
of republican rectitude. Pagnol's father and his uncle lived out, day
by day, the aged, formalised struggle between Church and State,
while sharing, as neutral middle ground, a passion for hunting. He
is as much a historian as a consummate artist; and his ears are at-
tuned to the stumbling language of childhood, his eyes to the
vagaries of southern spelling. He can recapture the engaging and
convoluted logic of childish observation. From the wonderful
freedom of the hills, he brings us down to the enclosed walled
territory of the gloomy *cour d'école*; and no French author has been
more successful in a genre that might be described as *le roman
scolaire*, the memory of irregular verbs and of grammatical conun-
drums, in a dangerously exact language—and goodness knows how
heavily *la scolarité* must have weighed on the lives of French
children—and of their parents—in the golden years of the
République des professeurs. But he is also a magician who can trans-
form the heavily formal parc Borély into a realm of wonder, and a
grinding tram into a vehicle of the Far West.

He is aware that country people seldom undress and rarely wash all over; and he senses the timid reticence of the little peasant boy when expected to undress completely in front of the fire, in the presence of grown-ups, a shyness not shared by his urban friend. Washing habits still represent one of the great dividing-lines between the urban and the rural child, just as, before 1914, there still remains a tremendous gulf between town and country, even though Lili's father may come right down into Marseilles once or twice a week, to sell his fruit at one of the open markets. He comes as a stranger, in haste to get back to the secretive community of the heights. Much of the magical quality of the hinterland, visible even from the prison of the school-yard, is that it is both so close to the city and yet normally so unattainable; Marseilles is perhaps unique in that it stops all at once on the edge of an aromatic desert and that wild animals roam within sight of its enveloping *faubourgs*.

But Pagnol is a lone witness of Marseilles. And apart from him, in the south generally, only the novelist Marc Bernard, in five or six novels, can recall the children of the ancient Roman town of Nîmes. Children, Protestant and Catholic, already conscious at school of their religious differentiations and living, indeed, in distinctive quarters of the town: the Protestants outside the area of the town (once surrounded by walls and ramparts, now surrounded by a circular boulevard), because the recalcitrant Protestants were not allowed to live within city limits before the Edict of Toleration of 1787; the Catholic population, generally of a lower economic status, are living in the old quarters, in the shadow of the cathedral and within the walls of the town. Children, quite conscious of belonging to two religious communities that historically could look back to two or three centuries of most dreadful violence, had, in the happier times following 1830, become accustomed one to another; and, after all, they would all speak with the same very marked Nîmois accent. They would also be enclosed in a warm and common populism. Bernard is very much a populist writer, looking forward to outings to the two nearest points on the sea, Le Grau-du-Roi and what always seems to me to be the rather bizarrely named Palavas-les-flots.

A childhood also echoing to the music, the vigorous music, of the Salvation Army—l'Armée du Salut, the French officer corps of which has always largely been monopolised by Nîmois—to the vigorous hymns of the Pentecostal Brethren, les Frères de la Pentecôte, as well as to the hymns of Jean Calvin and his successors, Nîmes not being just the Calvinist capital of France, but the capital of every imaginable Protestant group, even including the Mormons, les Témoins de Jéhovah, and so on and so forth. And, in Bernard's novels, a childhood extended, strengthened, and reinforced by a very early sense of belonging to a small, loving, very proud, extended family; a family that would reach out northwards to the very poor, almost inaccessible mountainous areas of what is called *le pays cévenol*, the heartland of French Protestantism, *Le Val sans issue*, which took the Maréchal Villars and an army of 2,000 Swiss to break down a resistance there, in 1708; a family also extending out to Geneva, Lausanne—the seat of the old Académie de Lausanne which gave seventeenth- and eighteenth-century France most of its underground *pasteurs*—extending even to Edinburgh. What Bernard called, and other French Protestants still call, *la Grande Famille*—the family of what both Protestants and Catholics will sometimes call the R.P.R., *la Religion Prétendue Réformée*.

At quite a different social level, Evelyne Sullerot, in a series of essays about childhood (she is, in fact, more of a literary critic than a novelist), can recall the white dresses, the sunny tennis-parties, and the old ladies in hats and veils generally wearing white or yellow rather than black—black would be the colour of the old and more widely accepted religion in France—as they come out of the whitewashed Protestant *temples*, shining in the very luminous light of the Atlantic Coast, in La Rochelle and in the villages of the two Charentes.

Can maturity, coupled with exile, have emphasised and exaggerated Albert Camus' oppressive (you can almost feel it) evocation of extreme and torrid heat, a heat that is almost humming? The utter immobility of a 3 p.m. sky under the burning sun of a small beach off one of the bays, one of the *corniches*, just to the east of the tiered white-and-green city of Algiers. I am thinking of *L'Étranger* and of the scene of the murder in *L'Étranger*. This, of course, is not so much innocence recaptured as the stupor produced by heat and by an angry, coarse wine—Mascara or some other of those earthy wines of the Algerian vineyards. Yet Camus' young man, *l'étranger*, a young man who has lost his way, is, in fact, very deeply embedded in his native city, which is also Camus' city, and in the peculiarly hybrid language and culture of the lower-middle-class settler community, *les petits pieds noirs*. And he is also deeply embedded in an alternance of work and leisure common to a whole class of European *petits employés* in what had been at one time and was, until fifteen years ago, a European city as well as an Arab city, a European city made up of an extraordinary mixture of French, mostly from the South of France, Maltese, Spanish, Italians from southern Italy, speaking a weird mixture of all these languages, *la langue de Cagayous*—the noisy world of Cagayous, a sort of people's philosopher—now, of course, lost and, within the course of the next generation, likely to be completely forgotten. Already, the downtown lower-middle-class European quarters of Algiers—Bab'l-Oued and Belcour—seem almost as remote to us as Sidi-Bel-Abbès, the legendary headquarters of the Foreign Legion, or, indeed, as remote as the French-speaking upper-middle-class, upper bourgeoisie of the old Wafd Party that, thirty years ago, still dominated the cultural life and polite society and café society of Cairo, wearing Savile Row suits, wearing fezzes, and sitting on café terraces reading *Le Journal du Caire* and sending their children to the Lycée Français du Caire or *lycées* in Paris or elsewhere in France.

Colonialism is no doubt a very wicked thing; it is certainly a very unfashionable thing, the disappearance of which is not to be regretted. Yet one must remember, I think, that it produced an evocative literature which was quite of its own, very rich in exoticism, in brilliant colours, and, of course, in a very early sense of hopelessness and despair. How little, for instance, would Marguerite Duras amount to as a writer, had she not had a childhood in the rice-fields of the Mekong Delta in Indo-China to draw upon? Her mother was a widow, her father had been in the French Indo-Chinese Customs, and the family was left with a tiny rice-farm that her mother, her brother, and a single Indo-Chinese farm-hand attempted to run. They lived in constantly impecunious circumstances and, in one of her novels, there is a very brilliant recall of this peculiar geography and this peculiar childhood. The more distant the place of childhood, remembered in the alien north of Paris, the brighter the colours, and the darker the greens, and the more brilliant the reds and the yellows and the more luxuriant the bougainvillaeas and the more peppery the smell of rot and decay.

Think of such writers, writing in French although having British nationality because they were from Mauritius, as Loÿs Masson, or the female novelist Alix d'Unienville—a marvellously Norman and seventeenth-century name, incidentally, such as characterises so many of the older French families of what the French still call l'Île Maurice—repainting an unbelievably vivid childhood and adolescence in Mauritius, l'Île Maurice and le Jockey Club de l'Île Maurice, and the sort of upper 200 of l'Île Maurice; now an independent republic which is barely recognisable as French-speaking, Urdu and Hindi and Chinese having swamped both the small number of original French families, and the much larger number of the local population who still speak a sort of creolised French—*le français créole de l'Île Maurice*.

Childhood, or at least childhood recollected, as I said before, no doubt with conscious, or perhaps unconscious, selectivity, is certainly the best possible framework for the exploration of time and of place, because its scope is both limited—it is often limited to that of the maximum distance likely to be covered by an eight-year-old boy or girl on foot, or on bicycle by a fourteen-year-old; this, after all, when you think of it, represents the full and yet extraordinarily mysterious topography of *Le Grand Meaulnes*—also because it is enclosed in a slow-moving, predictable, and immensely reassuring daily calendar. A day which one could compartmentalise between waking up—or better still, being woken up—the sun streaming into a bedroom (those early scenes in Proust, for instance, in Combray), or the excitement of waking up to look at the bedroom ceiling, and find it is an unusually pallid white, announcing the whiteness of a heavy fall of snow outside, or waking up to see the window streaming with rain. And so the day goes on: getting dressed, breakfast, and then the whole day divided up into neat sections, each section marked by a meal, as well as by the changing light, changing sensations of warmth and cold, and culminating in the nautical adventure and great waves—truly Palavas-les-flots in this case—provided by a bath, tucking up in bed, a story read before sleep, and the utter safety of the bedroom, with its familiar noises and friendly shadows moving about on walls and ceilings. A miniature world of innocence, but also of cunning, a miniature world which is never entirely abandoned, a miniature world still enveloping the adolescent or the adult, in moments of fear or bewilderment, as an experience of a treasure of wonder and discovery, the acute, the very acute, physical and aural perceptions of the very young.

3

Death and the Family

I deliberately dawdled on the subject of childhood because—in terms of evocation, attention to detail, the memory of detail, the awareness of colour, and so the awareness of very subtle things like period, as illustrated, for instance, in a change of clothing, or a change of period—childhood is, I suppose, the period in life in which one is the most perceptive. One may notice this, for instance, in those novels of Beryl Bainbridge which are undoubtedly situated in the immediate post-war period because some of the characters are still wearing A.R.P. badges or helmets, and so on. For this reason, I thought it was necessary to take childhood rather slowly, as, indeed, childhood appears to a child: a period of one's life that moves very, very slowly.

But, of course, childhood cannot last us very long, even in evocation; one has to move on, first of all, to the usual great divides in any family history. Perhaps this is more so in France than in most other Western European countries: the First Communion, prizegiving, the *bachot*, military service, marriage, or—jumping straight away to the very other end—death, burial, a family funeral. Here again one has the means, as it were, of stopping the clock, very briefly, and seeing an extended family reunited almost as if in a photographer's print. And, as Theodore Zeldin so constantly reminds us in his remarkable study of modern France, perhaps the one unit that has kept a divisive French society together, in the late nineteenth century and in this century, is that of the family—the family in death as much as the family at birth, at a wedding—the family in life.

And so I think of a number of novels which are formalised around the business of disposing of the dead; the business, also, of making all the right gestures, often quite formal gestures, to keep one's place in society among the living—in one's street, in one's neighbourhood, in one's profession. I would start off with the rather wretchedly proletarian novel by Paul Nizan, a former member of the French Communist Party who is probably much better known as the author of that marvellous political novel about the

1930s, *La Conspiration*. Nizan's account, a very drably Marxist
account, is of the death of his father, who was, all his life, a
railwayman, *un employé de la S.N.C.F.*, in some bureaucratic
capacity. (He was not an engine-driver or a fireman, but more
somebody who would wear a peaked cap, perhaps not a stationmaster, but a deputy stationmaster, or something of that kind, employed on one of the western lines, in the west of France.) His death
takes place in a villa in some rather sad, very silent, little town. The
silence is, somehow, even heightened by the circumstances;
something has been put down in the street to lessen the sound of
passing carts. Certainly, a very sad place, wherever it is. It might be
Poitiers, but I do not think it is; more likely Niort, Angoulême, or
perhaps Loudun. The street is small, in fact, an *impasse* or, as we
might say, a cul-de-sac, with a row of three-storeyed villas with
iron shutters. In the villa where the man has died, the floors of the
front room, the *salon*, have been rewaxed, the curtains have been
drawn, and the street itself is utterly silent, as if in sympathy or
complicity, but, in fact, more in fear and curiosity: the ultimate
resignation of a life which totals up to resignation.

Antoine Bloyé is a novel which has been described as one of the
very rare proletarian novels of French literature, in which the central character is the dead man, and only peripherally his family, his
widow, the neighbours, relatives, and so on. It is really a novel
about the increasing ripples of the awareness of death: first of all, in
the house itself, with the unusual silence, the lack of the usual
movements. In the street outside, there is again the lack of
movement. There are rather timid ringings on the bell, and neighbours, one after another, come to present their *condoléances*. And
then follows the collective and professional grief of the various
associates of the dead man; and, finally, the feelings of his *proches*,
of his children in particular. It is an extraordinary evocation of one
of those very silent and rather sad towns in the west of France.

Then there is Roger Peyrefitte's novel about the death of his
mother, which he calls *La Mort d'une mère*, in a nursing-home, in a
clinique, run by nuns. There are more waxed floors and, again,
silence broken by whispering. The nursing-home is in a very quiet
avenue beyond the old university in the seventeenth-century and the
mediaeval part of Toulouse, in the neighbourhood of Saint-Sernin
and the rue du Taur. Much of this novel is on the subject not just of
Toulouse and the writer's childhood, but also of guilt because, on a
number of previous occasions, he had received telegrams from the

Mother Superior of the nursing-home in which his mother, now very old, was being looked after: '*Mère au plus mal.*' Each time, he takes the train to or he flies to Toulouse and then, time and time again, his mother, a very sturdy old lady, recovers. On this occasion, therefore, when he receives the standard telegram from the Mother Superior, he decides to ignore it, in order to attend some very important literary function in Paris; so he puts off his journey to the south-west for 48 hours and, when he does eventually go to Toulouse, he goes too late.

All the funerals that you could ask for and that seem always to take place in summer, in damp heat and rather rancid rancour, among the yellow-faced, black-draped figures of Mauriac's awful, suppurating, inbred Bordeaux. They are funerals in which there seems to have been very little room for love, but in which there are many hints of poison.

We can also have a very splendid family gathering, in one of those crenellated baronial halls—Moorish style, pseudo-Alhambra, Château-de-Blois style, Scottish baronial, Arab style, various Spanish styles, minor Notre-Dame style—the extraordinary range of exoticism favoured by the wool barons in the wool town of Roubaix, in the wide avenues off the municipal park, the Parc Barbieux, on the road to Lille. One such occasion was for the funeral of M. Achille, as he was known to his relatives and to all his employees, in a novel, *Rüdig,* written under a pseudonym (François Durban) by Robert Wibaux, himself a wool baron and, at one time, director of a very long-established wool firm, Filature Wibaux-Florin et Compagnie.

The occasion is a marvellous literary contrivance for reuniting, around the body of *l'ancien*, M. Achille, every branch of one of those extensive and closely intermarried textile families of Roubaix—Tourcoing. There are two or three generations: those who have remained in industry (or, as they would say in Roubaix, *dans l'industrie*, because there is only one industry and therefore it is *the* industry); those married *into* the industry; priests, monks, and nuns, younger brothers and sisters, therefore expendable on such vocations, *l'industrie* having been provided for by elder brothers and by suitable marriages on the part of elder sisters; those who still live in the neighbourhood, those who look after branch offices of the firm in other wool towns, in Mulhouse or in the south-west, in Mazamet; those who have recently come back from studying the technology of wool in Bradford, and, very often, with

quite a strong Yorkshire accent in French; those who have come
back from several years as purchasers in Australia, often with quite
distinctive Australian accents in French. And there are perhaps even
one or two rebellious natures, who have deviated away from *l'industrie*, and away from the church and the convent and the
monastery, into political or academic life, or those who have opted
for the highest ranks of state bureaucracy, even providing, of
course, for one or two total or near-failures—people, brothers,
cousins, and so on, seldom referred to and only seen on such extraordinary occasions. Gamblers, adventurers, drinkers, or perhaps
a man of whom it would be said that he was *criblé de femmes*, are,
all at once, readmitted, on an entirely temporary basis, into the intimacy of the clan, on the clear understanding that, once the body
of M. Achille has been disposed of with due pomp, such *brebis
galeuses* will then return to the conveniently distant localities of
their disgrace—probably to Paris, possibly to South America. The
sort of invitation put out for such an occasion would be like a pack
of cards, giving every possible permutation of marriage of the
twenty-odd families of the wool barons of Roubaix—Tourcoing.

Ever since, in the late nineteenth century, Henri Monnier wrote
his one-act play about a rural funeral, *L'Enterrement*, French
novelists have been more aware, I think, than those of other
nationalities of the unique possibilities offered by a funeral as a
literary device: to assemble, at one time and in one place, a very
large cast of characters, many of whom will not have seen one
another for very many years, a great many of whom will not have
been on speaking terms for a great many years, over some conflict
or another involving one or two *notaires* and last wills and
testaments and so on, and then to project the assemblage of
relations backwards in time.

Death and its accompaniments thus provide a theme especially
suited to the regional novel, regionalism expressing itself the most
vigorously and the most persistently through the great bourgeois
families of the north and the east of France. At a purely populist
level, it is much more rarely evoked. Perhaps simply because *un enterrement de troisième classe* offers far fewer possibilities, in terms
of a crowded cast, than one of the very first category. And, indeed,
un enterrement de quatrième classe could witness, at most, half a
dozen people—the window or the children, and a couple of rather
rubicund and generally extremely hilarious employees of the
pompes funèbres, a profession which seems always, in my ex-

perience, to lend itself to copious libations, rather loud voices, red faces, and a great deal of laughter. None the less, even that is a theme that has been exploited, against the Parisian suburban background in the middle of the 1930s, by the populist writer Eugène Dabit, in his short novel which simply covers three days, from 3 to 5 January, and is called *Un Mort tout neuf*.[1]

But who is going to invoke the *H.S.P.*, the *haute société protestante*, of Geneva, in its stronghold in the rue des Granges, at the top end of the old town? No Swiss writer really has dared. And so we have to fall back on a celebrated murder trial of the late 1950s, *l'affaire Jaccoud*, perhaps more expressive of that closed, self-satisfied, and secretive society even than the works of Lyons novelists on the subject of what goes on behind the closed and shuttered façades, the blind, blank walls in Ainay and Perrache at the bottom end of Lyons, like those of a line of brothels or a line of morgues or of the discreet houses of torture in the rue Lauriston in Paris—façades that will give absolutely nothing away and that do not even require the additional deterrent, '*chien méchant*'.

L'affaire Jaccoud was followed with very close attention by Georges Simenon. In one of his autobiographical pieces, he claims that, after reading very closely *Le Journal de Genève* and the other local reports of this astonishing family affair, he used much of the material for one of his very rare novels placed in French-speaking, Protestant Switzerland.[2] But he is not at home with its characters in the way he is with his artisan or shopkeeper characters, whether he places them in Belgium or Paris or in the west of France or wherever. This is possibly explained in terms of Simenon's own very obvious Catholic undertones in nearly all of his writing—the sights and sounds of Sunday and memories of childhood, memories, particularly, of his own childhood as an altar boy, of his own religious education in Liège—and he peoples a great many of his stories with young men who have missed their way, but who will evoke a similar childhood.

---

[1] 1934. The book is dedicated to that great historian of Paris and of Parisians, Louis Chevalier.

[2] In *La Mort de Belle*, in fact written in 1952, long before the *affaire* and before Simenon settled in the canton de Vaud, he seemed to foretell the case. *L'affaire Jaccoud* (a leading barrister, of French origin, and literary personality of the *H.S.P.* of Geneva) was a celebrated case of murder that has never been entirely elucidated. Jaccoud was accused, and convicted, of having murdered the father of his mistress, a nurse, in a lakeside villa. Simenon certainly followed the case very closely and may have used it for one of his later Maigrets.

Death can be very sordid in Simenon, as an occasion which reveals all sorts of previously hidden antipathies or family secrets, and this sort of thing, but it is never entirely sordid and, I think, always with Simenon, there is a very Catholic feeling about death—remorse, guilt, atonement—and, indeed, about the very comforting presence of maybe a parish priest or a nun or mother superior. I think this is never more apparent than in one of the last things he has written, which was really inspired by the death of his mother, who died well on into her nineties and who constantly refused to move from the small three-storeyed house in which she had always lived in the Quartier d'Outremeuse in Liège. Simenon was always saying, 'Why don't you come and live with me?' or, 'Why don't you live in Switzerland?' but she would not. Simenon describes her funeral and describes the various people whom, in the last twenty or thirty years of her life, she had seen—nuns, neighbours, shopkeepers, and so on—so that his book is one which is very different, really, from Peyrefitte's.

One feels that Peyrefitte is writing his book in order to get his own sense of guilt out of his system—perhaps not so much guilt as annoyance. 'Why wasn't I there? If I'd only gone there twenty-four hours earlier, I'd have been in time; it would have been all right.' There is irritation: his mother had somehow played this last trick on him, and this was very inconsiderate of her; she could have held out a little longer.

In Simenon's case, this is something quite different. His love for his extraordinary, aged mother and the strange, ambivalent relationship between himself and this very simple woman, who never really accustomed herself to the fact of her son's becoming a millionaire; in fact, she was always rather shocked by it and did not wish it, in any way, to change her own extremely austere and immobile way of life. Her son's book is, on the part of a man already in his seventies, a re-exploration of his own childhood and, at the same time, an act of *pietas* towards a lower-middle-class woman who had had a very hard life, had lost her husband very early, had never really been accepted in the huge family of her in-laws, who was herself linguistically of Dutch-German origin, from that very curious hotchpotch around Eupen and Malmédy, where three frontiers are sort of mixed up. In a sense, it is a piece of social history as well as a *témoignage* on the part of Simenon towards the person for whom he always felt the greatest affection and, on occasions perhaps, a certain amount of guilt, because he had, many times, tried to associate his mother with his own more spectacular triumphs—when he was given the civic freedom of his native city of Liège, and this sort of thing—and his mother really did not want to have anything to do with them. She would always say, '*Mon petit Georges, de telles choses, ce ne sont pas pour moi.*' And so, to some extent, I suppose she was a sort of living reproach, in that she was not prepared to partake in this success and thus to give it, as it were, her benediction.

This theme is very important to one's understanding of Georges Simenon, his whole attitude to life, which is a very pessimistic one. He tends to believe in the sinfulness of people, particularly if they fall out of what he regards as their proper circuit, their proper community. For example, girls, in Simenon, would have been all right if they had not taken the train to Paris; young men would have been all right if they had stayed put, stayed in their local, regional, family, professional circle, and so on. I think much of this in Simenon has something to do with his own very strong sense of a Catholic childhood and, indeed, I would say, his particular brand of Christianity.

Raymond Queneau is certainly a novelist who is very difficult to place, in this important respect, either from the religious point of view or any other. In his novels, death is quite incidental, really very peripheral. Take the death by accident in *Le Chiendent*, for instance. The old lady has the immense satisfaction of seeing a young man being run over, squashed to death, by a number 38 bus outside the Gare du Nord, and is so impressed by this that, for weeks afterwards, she goes every day and sits outside on a *terrasse de café* facing on to the Gare du Nord, hoping that the same thing will happen again. It does not happen again, but such is her optimism that she goes back, again and again; and this accident really furnished her old age, was a sort of enrichment for her.

This is one example of the way Queneau treats death, as something almost comical, but he can also deal with death in a manner which is marvellously discreet, almost polite. In *Pierrot mon ami*, one of the central figures is a very strange old man whose profession is making waxworks and who lives alone in a curiously isolated Louis-Philippe villa in a suburban street made up of garages, tanneries, junk-yards, and a very tiny little triangular cemetery which is built around a single chapel: the sort of landscape that very much pleases Queneau. The old man takes up with the young man (Pierrot), befriends him, and he wants to leave him a certain number of objects in the villa, and he says to him one day: 'I'd like you to come back in a day or two. Don't come tomorrow, because I might not be dead by tomorrow, but come back, say, in two days' time because, in two days' time, I will have had time, I think I will have had time, to have, you know, gone through that particular transformation—*de procéder à cette transformation*.' I find this a very endearing way of describing one's own physical process of death, on the part of somebody who feels that he is about to die, and it is very much, I think, in the line of Queneau's rather discreet humour.

It reminds me of a very discreet literary piece of inventiveness on the part of Chateaubriand, when he describes the dreadful circumstances of the kidnapping, the court-martialling, and then the execution of the duc d'Enghien—kidnapped in Germany, brought to Paris, midnight court-martial in the Château de Vincennes, shot in one of its empty moats—a process, I suppose, which can be put into twenty-four hours or a little bit more, and which Chateaubriand deliciously describes as *'le dépêchement du prince'*.

4

Barracks and the Military Novel

French literature, unlike our own, provides a further level of exposure to regional experience: a level that lies somewhere about a quarter of the way from childhood to disappointment, then perhaps the bitterness of failure or semi-failure, old age, and death. It is the level of military service, which is a stage as inevitable, almost as natural, in the normal progression of a masculine life, as birth, First Communion, the successful culmination of *le baccalauréat*, marriage, one child, then perhaps several more children, perhaps even culminating in the *carte de priorité*, given to *un père de famille nombreuse*.

In fact, it is a level of experience which is so firmly set in masculine national experience as to form one photograph in a series of rather formal photographs, each one of which represents one of these peaks, or perhaps one might say troughs, in a conventional masculine existence. No French biography could be complete without the subject of the biography being, as it were, *encadré*, in the framework, of *la photo du régiment*.[1] For instance, Raymond Queneau photographed during his military service in Algeria, in the *tirailleurs algériens*, an experience which gave him the broom, the *balai*, an instrument to which he returns lovingly in many of his novels—*le balai, le balayage,* and so on—so much of a recruit's life being occupied with sweeping out a barrack-square or a barrack-room.

Perhaps this is hardly the place to discuss military service, which, in design if not in practice, was meant to provide the very antithesis of regionalism, being supposed, particularly in the eyes of the republican, anti-clerical people, before the First World War, who would describe themselves as left protagonists, as an effort to de-regionalise the conscript in the common bondage of the long barrack-room dormitory: what so many French pre-1914 pamphleteers and politicians called *l'école du soldat, l'école du*

---

[1] 'A cette époque [that is, about 1910] une photographie était un document remarquable, qui perpétuait le souvenir de la première enfance, du service militaire, d'un mariage, ou d'un voyage à étranger . . .' (Marcel Pagnol, *La Gloire de mon père*).

citoyen.[1] It was therefore also seen as an educational encouragement, indeed stronghold, of the French language; the unity of the French language, the universality of the French language, *la langue française, une et indivisible*, as against the various patois that had survived in France in a predominantly peasant society up to 1914, and, indeed, the various minority languages which had survived up till then. No doubt that it was this in one respect, and certainly in the intention of many of those, both of the left and right, who remained fervent partisans of compulsory military service. Yet, on the other hand, military service produced its own literature—a literature which is *militaire* rather than militaristic, or, on the contrary, which could be anti-militarist; that is to say, a very early literary form of protest and exasperation very much affected by anarchist and pacifist writers, and dating back to the second half of the 1890s: I think it is very significant that the Dreyfus affair coincides with the publication in France of the first really effective anti-military novels.

Military service literature is one that creates its own topography as well as its own language, its own *hauts lieux* and *bas lieux*, its own geographical *grandeurs et servitudes*: Metz, Strasbourg, Châlons-sur-Marne, Suippes, Bar-le-Duc, Toul, Verdun; then, later on, the hugely complex geography, underground and above ground, of *la ligne Maginot*—a predominantly eastern topography, a topography which remains associated with dark pine forests, extreme cold, the towpaths of dreary, straight canals, and with a landscape of desolation. There is the terrible boredom, accentuated by confinement to a very narrow urban precinct, and, of course, by chronic shortage of money, given the lamentably low pay of the French recruit at any time during this period. A couple of streets just beyond the barracks (themselves generally placed with other *établissements insalubres*, like sewage-farms, gasworks, cemeteries, slaughterhouses, chemical works, on the periphery of the town, well away from the centre, even more from the residential quarters) is a line of cafés, brothels, all of them constantly packed, particularly towards the end of the week, with long queues before each one on Friday and on Saturday nights.

---

[1] A school in a more general sense, in which the countryman might be exposed to urban tastes and might even have his most firmly entrenched eating habits extended to include exotic food and fruit. '. . . Quand nous en fûmes aux bananes, il pela la sienne en disant: "ça, j'en ai déjà mangé à Marseille au service militaire." ' This from François, a peasant living in the wild *garrigue* above the city. (Marcel Pagnol, *Le Temps des secrets*.)

Equally grim are the *sou*-less walks along bleak canals lined with heartless and hopeless trees, as if out on parade to remind the hapless conscript that there is no escape from the imperatives of the sergeant-major, the literary sergeant-major, the proverbial *l'adjudant Flick*.

If the poor young soldier is lucky, there will be encounters with willing local girls on the steep flanks of Vauban-designed ramparts, squares, hexagons, diamonds, *triples enceintes*—dark monuments in ancient stone covered in parsimonious, dirty grass and offering very little comfort, very little hold.

A Frenchman will say, when talking about himself, '*J'ai fait mon service à Toul*,' '*Bar-le-Duc*', '*Châlons*', '*Suippes*,' wherever it happens to be. Or '*du temps où je faisais mon service*'. Notice the use of the imperfect as something that is so habitual as to be common pretty well to every Frenchman. Or '*Après avoir fait mon service je suis rentré à Paris*', or wherever it is, '*et je me suis établi*,' in such-and-such a job, such-and-such a profession, and then maybe, '*m'etant établi, je me suis marié.*' There is, equally, an entirely immutable geography, what I would describe as Courtelinesque geography—the geography of the many, comic for the readers, perhaps not so much for the participants, barrack novels of the great late nineteenth-century French humorist Georges Courteline: *Le Train de huit heures quarante-sept*, etc. etc. There is a completely changeless Courtelinesque geography, approached always by trains from the Gare de l'Est, and not from the Gare du Nord, and ending in the desperation of Bar-le-Duc, Haguenau, Wissembourg, Bitche, Sélestat. One wonders, sometimes, why France so much wished to recover, after 1870, so hopeless a topography, a topography which suitably leaves from the Gare de l'Est, at which, until the Second World War, the central departure platforms used to be surmounted by an enormous allegorical picture, a very depressing one, at least to myself, and I think probably to most people who were travelling in that direction, representing a departure of troop trains sometime in 1915 or 1916.

One could propose another, similar, set topography, one which would depart from the Gare de Lyon to Marseilles, thence by ship to Algiers, Oran, Constantine, Tunis, Casablanca, and so on, and beyond, to the brilliant white and green of Sidi-bel-Abbès, which inevitably figures in any novel concerned with the Foreign Legion, Sidi-bel-Abbès being the Legion's depot from the time of its foundation to the time it was withdrawn with Algerian independence. The Legion still maintains a southern topography even today: its main depot is in Aubagne, the birthplace of Pagnol, just outside Marseilles.

If a soldier fell into some sort of military disrepute, he was sent to the terrible stony deserts of south Tunisia, to what the French call *biribi*, the *compagnies de discipline*, the area of cruel military punishment of the really bad or undisciplined soldiers. A brief air of exoticism is thus lent to Parisians, Lillois, Bretons, and Tourangeaux nostalgically recalling, later in life, a few Arab words, particularly during the sort of chance encounters one has on the platform of a bus or in the Métro, etc., with references to the hennaed Ouled-Nail girls, and the doubtful charms of the *B.M.A.*, the *bordel militaire ambulant*, which was used by the French colonial army in North Africa, and illustrated with a very slight sprinkling of what are supposed to be borrowings from Arabic: *mena-mena*, *barka*, *fissa*, etc.—a device which was used with great affection and effectiveness, I think, by Raymond Queneau in a number of his novels. And, indeed, the experience of military service in North Africa has brought quite a considerable number of Arab words into the common French vocabulary. I suppose the one that will spring to mind immediately to anybody is that of *toubib*, a military doctor, which finally, by a process of general application, has become a slang word for doctor.

It is a topography which is so formal, and so changeless, and which has such very clearly defined frontiers, as to provide in advance the rough framework of a score or more of military novels; humoristic, nostalgic, bitter, tragic, rancorous, or even vaguely tender, in the rather rough and very masculine tenderness of fraternity and common discomfort and shared danger, and which, at times, can be stretched to include, in this century, the exotic-sounding Plaine des Jarres, the Mekong Delta, and the many-mirrored but rather expensive joys of Cholon, the brothel and pleasure quarter of Saigon. In fact, I think part of the attraction of this most formal type of military novel—and the most formal type really belongs to the pre-1914 period—is the reassuring immutability of the geography.

It is very well illustrated in one of Queneau's middle novels, *Le Dimanche de la vie*, the hero of which is a long-service, volunteer soldier in a colonial regiment, who has reached, I think, one stripe, possibly two stripes, and whose knowledge of French geography is limited to the place he was born in—the suburbs of Paris, one of those suburbs of incredibly banal-sounding names of which Queneau is particularly fond: Bécon-les Bruyères, or somewhere like that. The personal geography of this soldier, Valentin Bru, is, let us say, Aubervilliers, north of Paris—his birthplace. The Gare de Lyon is from where he travels in a train for the first time in his life, to join his regimental depot, in Marseilles. He leaves Marseilles, for a series of garrisons in Morocco, Algeria, and Tunisia. He returns to France by a different route, via Bordeaux, where the colonial dispersal centre is in a suburb outside the city, Le Bouscat. On his demobilisation, he travels in a train for the second time in his life—back to Paris.

The military novel will also have imposed upon it an equally inevitably limited range of characters, dominated nearly always by that of *l'adjudant-chef*, the French equivalent of a regimental sergeant-major. He is always the central figure, the demon figure in many ways. He will have certain verbal, facial characteristics; he will be heavily moustached.

Then there will be an exceedingly amorous captain: there are innumerable jokes about the amorous activities of *le capitaine un tel*, almost as much a formalised figure as the types one gets in British beach postcards of our own classic period of beach postcards. To offset the amorous captain, there is a lecherous *lieutenant* or a *sous-lieutenant*. Both officers are usually in the cavalry, in order, I suppose, to illustrate the theme that cavalry officers are more attractive to girls than those of any other corps, and that they use, in the pursuit of females, willing or unwilling, the same sort of *brio* as they are expected to use in a classical 1870-type cavalry charge, and, of course, are always represented as going to bed booted and spurred, much to the damage of the sheets.

The *adjudant-chef*, the *juteux*, will generally either be Corsican or Alsatian, and this will, of course, give the author very wide possibilities for taking off his manner of speech, with the Italo-French of the Corsicans or the Germano-French of the classic Alsatian comic character, unable to pronounce the French 'g': if he wants to say '*gardien*,' he will say '*cartien*'. This sort of thing is always good for a laugh. It makes very, very little difference whether he is the standard Corsican or the standard Alsatian sergeant-major. Whichever he is, he will always be loud-mouthed, bullying, and malevolent in an unimaginative way. For example, the malevolence which consists in a play on words: 'What was your civilian profession? Oh, artist—well, you can go and draw that

watercart.' Similar and equally much-used turns of speech and so
on attributed to French sergeant-majors include: '*Vous êtes artiste,
vous pouvez donc être artiste des chiottes.*'

The rest of the plot will then fall into place around such terribly
worn and hackneyed themes as punishment, confined to barracks,
sweeping out the yard, so that Valentin Bru, when he is talking to
his friend the sergeant, and contemplating what he is going to do in
civilian life, says: 'I'm very drawn to sweeping—*le balayage, voilà
un métier qui a de l'avenir*—I think, even with industrialisation and
improved techniques, the old-fashioned broom will still be in
demand. What is particularly interesting in this highly technical
job are *les petits coins*—the little corners, the difficult pieces.' Of
course, in most such novels, the French army was still substantially
horse-drawn (*hippomobile*), thus lending a whole extra sphere of
work to the military sweeper, *le balayeur militaire*.

Amid the high spots, or low spots, of an imposed and compulsory military career, something that is waited upon longingly,
perhaps for weeks and months in advance, is *la permission*; that is
to say, leave. Something that is feared is *le rabiot*, having a period
added to one's military service as a result of some misbehaviour or
other. Always in the distance as the final liberation, rather like the
sun at the end of a Charlie Chaplin film, seen at the end of a very
long, long road, is demobilisation, what the French call *la quille*. I
do not know why it is called *la quille*, for *la quille* literally means a
ninepin. *La quille* has become so formalised in French military life,
language, and literature that, until quite recently, certainly at the
time of the Algerian war, one could go into almost any *tabac* in
Paris or any other French town and buy a particular sort of military
joke postcard which would have a circle attached to it which you
could pull round so that you would have on the top *à combien la
quille?* and you could then fix it at 30 days, two months, 15 days,
and so on. The idea was to send it to some young man who was
waiting for his number to come up, as it were—*la quille*.

If something gets into joke postcards, then it becomes as formalised a part of French life as were those photographs which were
very popular during the First World War, of soldiers photographed
against a photomontage background, so that they would appear to
be sitting in a very small-sized aeroplane or barrage balloon, or
something of that sort. Equally, of course, the brothel week-end
and a drunken sortie. In fact, it was a French preview of a genre of
humorous literature later adopted with enormous success by the

German writer H. H. Kirst, writing about the adventures of a mythical corporal in the Wehrmacht in the Second World War: Corporal Asch and his tribulations, mostly at the hands of his immediate superiors, with the inevitable and terrifying sergeant-major, and so on and so forth. I think it is interesting to note that Kirst, in French translation, has been almost as much a publisher's success as it has been in Germany, because, again, the topography is similar, though there are one or two things in Kirst that one does not find in Courteline, but which would, I think, have appealed to him; for example, very late Saturday-night, early Sunday-morning exercises in what you might call the parabola of urination—who could get it highest—and other similar masculine competitions.

As military humour, in French at least, mostly concerns an army that was horse-drawn, the French military novel and French military humour find their greatest fulfilment in the pre-1914 period, when shakos, those peculiar tall hats that one associates with Saint-Cyr, now Coëtquidam, with the French officer corps training, were worn, with blue tunics and red trousers. That very fixed military life was lovingly and brilliantly portrayed by René Clair, in one of his last films, *Les Grandes Manoeuvres*, which was about the intense boredom of military life somewhere in the doldrums of about 1900-1905, in some extremely boring town in the east or the north-east, like Bar-le-Duc. It was, indeed, a mirror, in its utter fixity, to the general complacency of what I would describe as the lush years of the Third Republic, say, 1890-1914. There would be very few recruits, though perhaps some officers, who might have had the courage, or even the imagination, to peer over the high, yellow wall of the barracks, and to seek escape in the backwaters of a contiguous civilian society.

Louis Rossel, a regular army officer, tried. His mother was a Scottish woman, from Edinburgh, and his father a member of an old Protestant family from Nîmes: a double heritage which may possibly account for the pigheadedness of this unfortunate man, who, having become, out of patriotism, the chief of staff to the Paris Commune, was tried by court-martial after the collapse of the Commune and shot, in 1871. During his first garrison duties, in Metz, in the 1850s, Rossel sought out, first of all, the local *pasteur*, to whom he had an introduction. Then he was driven, perhaps in sheer desperation, but more likely, I think, out of a natural pedagogic bent, to attend the meetings of the local *société savante*, or the *société d'archéologie*, or the *société messine d'émulation*, or the *société messine de géographie*, or whatever it was called.

I do not think, however, one can take Rossel as a typical example; I mean, he was a very odd fellow, and he was perhaps a born nonconformist. Most soldiers would have trodden the weary path from barracks to brothel, from brothel to café, everlastingly mulling over, with a companion, the latest iniquity of the *adjudant-chef*, or the latest amorous exploit of the *lieutenant* or the *sous-lieutenant*; a form, indeed, of voyeurism to be enjoyed at several removes of circumstance and rank by those who could not afford it.

So much, then, for what I would call a *roman militaire*, the *humour de la caserne* and, indeed, on the other side, the *littérature antimilitariste*, which, because it is obsessive, strident, and angry, can never be really great literature. So much, again, for the insistent topography of eastern France. When all is said and done, however, reading books in these categories is an experience which is possibly enriching, from the literary point of view at least, because it is one which almost every French male, at least until the 1960s, could share in, and of which, however unwittingly and unhappily, he could feel a part: it was *his* scene, even though it was a scene that had been imposed upon him. And for this reason alone, it must, of course, always remain, as a literary form, a literature atrophied and amputated, in that it is not only essentially masculine, a man's world for men only, but it tends to be contemptuous of women, reducing them merely to the role of extremely summary, and necessarily inexpensive, *machines à plaisir*.

So, in this respect, again, I think this form of literature is very much a period piece, contemporaneous with a hundred years or so of middle-class history in which, in the political and public sphere at least, although not in the family sphere, masculine attitudes were not only prevalent, but were also firmly entrenched, in law and habit, above all, in the *code civil* and the *code pénal*. Their very entrenchment, though, in statute and in law often concealed the hidden sources of feminine influence, particularly within the family, and particularly regarding the education of children, and, above all, that of daughters. Certainly, it is very hard to see what a woman would find to amuse her in Georges Courteline, or, indeed, to horrify and repel her in such anti-military novels as Henri Barbusse's *Le Feu*, and Dorgelès' *Les Croix de bois*, both leading anti-military, anti-war novels written about the First World War, by men who had had a direct and horrifying experience of long-drawn-out trench warfare, or in the anti-military colonial novels of a military misfit such as the novelist Georges Darien, who had taken on a long-term engagement in the French horsedrawn artillery and who ended up in the penal battalions in the deserts of south Tunisia, which resulted in his writing what is one of the classics of French anti-militarism, *Biribi*, on the subject of the appalling cruelty of the Bataillons d'Afrique, in French slang, *'bat' d'af'*; the French equivalent, I suppose, of what we would call the glasshouse.

There would, however, be compensations for the female reader of Raymond Radiguet's brilliant novel *Le Diable au corps*. First published in 1923, it is concerned with the sexual situation offered in Paris to a young adolescent, barely out of the *lycée,* by the absence of men and the presence of a slightly older generation of French women, and it represents, amongst other things, women's revenge on a series of standards imposed by men. Adult males might not be able to opt out of the war, the aims of which they may often have utterly rejected, but teenage males could, and did, profit from a field thus left open to them, just as Raymond Queneau's prowling bands of 15-year-old *morveux*, sons of dockworkers or of mobilised soldiers, did in the Le Havre of 1916.

And when one thinks of Radiguet, one also thinks of Cocteau's novel *Thomas l'imposteur*, the hero of which is somebody below the age of military service putting to good, individual, personal profit the unusual circumstances of a period of prolonged war, such as had been reached at the end of 1916 and the beginning of 1917.

Radiguet, almost alone, has attempted to tackle the rather delicate and dangerous subject of women in a military situation, though it had previously been alluded to in another of Darien's novels, *Bas les coeurs!*, which is a novel about Versailles during the Paris Commune, a novel which admirably represents the double standard laid by the conformists of patriotism on women. There is the poor professional prostitute who, during the period of Prussian occupation of Versailles, in 1870-71, has Prussian soldiers and N.C.O.s among her regular customers, and then is assaulted on the railway station at Versailles, beaten up with umbrellas by a lot of patriotic ladies, and, eventually, has her head shorn. There is the wife of a French cavalry officer who is a prisoner-of-war somewhere in Germany taking in a wounded Prussian officer who had been billeted upon her; actually, she did not take him in, but she did extend her hospital services to him to the most extreme measure that a woman could—but that was all right because she

was a lady. A very fine, interesting theme that has since been ven-
tilated by Marguerite Duras, in some of her novels.

In general, though, the French military novel represents a form
of literature which is almost as stultified and repetitive as the
equally masculine-dominated, provincial, and now somewhat
jaded Théâtre du Palais-Royal: *ménage à trois*—husband absent,
wife entertaining lover, unexpected return of husband, trouserless
lover hiding in the wardrobe; wardrobe tipping over; or trouserless
lover hiding under the bed, his feet sticking out, and returning
husband falling over them, and so on. It is a form of amusement,
one you might call *l'humour du cocuage*, the humour of cuckoldry,
which certainly represents one of the most characteristic types of
the literature of male chauvinism of the Third Republic, and indeed, one of the most characteristic types of middle-class, especially
provincial, literature of the Fifth Republic today. It is not entirely
dead, although, in a recent interview with a journalist from *Paris-
Match*, the present manager of the Théâtre du Palais-Royal said:
'Ah, things are not what they used to be; I have very, very few
customers now under the age of sixty, and most of those come from
Lyons, Bordeaux, and such places.'

Both the French military novel and the humour of cuckoldry are
really forms of masculine escape and fantasy, particularly for the
male who is middle-aged, who is at that dangerous period in
masculine life; what, in French literature and in French slang, is
referred to as *le démon de midi*, something that resides, I suppose,
in even the most pedestrian French provincial Homais—*phar-
macien*, veterinary surgeon, dentist, and so on.

Only the literature of total defeat and complete military disaster
can result in such an anarchical masterpiece as Lucien Rebatet's *Les
Décombres*, an extraordinarily powerful literary evocation of the
collapse of the French army in June 1940. Based on Rebatet's own
experiences, it is an almost vengeful and joyful representation of
the total demoralisation, indiscipline, and, above all, tremendous
alcoholism—*gros rouge* flowing, as the military situation gets
worse, in greater and greater quantities.

There is also the more recent anarchical literary masterpiece *Le
Roi des aulnes*, by Michel Tournier, one of the most remarkable
novels to come out of France in the last ten years and one that, for
once, was rightly honoured by being given the Prix Goncourt. In it,
Michel Tournier totally rejects the collective orthodoxy of the

French male, an orthodoxy that becomes more querulous, more insistent, more repetitive, and, ultimately, more intolerable with every successive kilometre of the journey eastwards as prisoners-of-war, in closed cattle-trucks. Eventually, when the cattle train reaches the deep forest lands of East Prussia, each prisoner-of-war has become, as it were, *fixé* in his chosen provincial role and his chosen professional attitude. The Parisien has become, with each kilometre eastwards, more *parisien*, his 'a's have become longer and more nostalgic; the Auvergnat has become more *auvergnat*; the Marseillais has become a sad parody of himself, his *galéjades*, his Canebière jokes become increasingly creaky; as, in those dark eastern lands, they endlessly act out the minutiae of an existence far removed and thus banally reassuring—something almost as sad as those many nostalgic films that one sees about Colditz, and about amateur dramatic performances in prisoner-of-war camps in Germany. It was also equally well represented in that marvellous classic of the French cinema *La Grande Illusion*, which refers to the extreme difficulty, in conditions of military captivity, of escaping out of the doubly narrow confines of your own national society.

The principal hero of Michel Tournier's novel, which, I suspect, is largely autobiographical, is not just the odd man out, a sort of twentieth-century Louis Rossel who dares to look over the barrack-wall, or, rather, over the barbed wire of the prisoner-of-war camp; he goes much farther than that. He withdraws totally from this confined and, of course, increasingly tattered trap of a national society and transfers, by slow, deliberate, methodical stages, into the attitudes and the highly mysterious geography of a completely alien national culture; and one could not imagine a national culture more completely alien to Tournier's hero, Tiffauges, who is from the Beauvaisis, than that of the dark forest lands of East Prussia, the land of the Junkers, of Hindenburg, of the great game preserves of Goering, of the very cradle of Prussian nationalism.

Tiffauges travels the whole distance. First of all, he is accepted as a skilled conservationist, to use the now fashionable word, by the foresters, gamekeepers, and hunters, all of them wearing the uniform and the emblem of Goering's immense East Prussian estates. He is not just accepted by these semi-military underlings, mostly men over military age, but he is also accepted by the deer, the foxes, the wild boar, the occasional lonely and rather scraggy wolf, the furry creatures, the birds of prey, the wild duck—the extraordinarily varied population of a hunter's paradise. Later on, he is accepted by the inhabitants of East Prussian villages and small market-towns.

Finally, he succeeds in penetrating the very inner sanctum of Nazism, its hope for the future, the guarantee of the Thousand Year Reich, an S.S. school set in an ancient castle of one of the Teutonic Knights. The S.S. school is an élite school, one where the boys, good-looking and racially pure, have all been very carefully vetted before being admitted. They have been recruited from among the lakes and forests of this Slavonic borderland (and so perhaps not *quite* so racially pure as they looked) at the age of twelve, totally re-equipped with clothes, including scarlet vests and underpants, then indoctrinated in extreme fanaticism and trained for early death. This French prisoner-of-war is given a horse, and he rides about what becomes, as it were, his own private kingdom, seeking out boys of the correct racial background, in order to bring them into the castle for induction into training in the S.S.—often, of course, very much against the wishes of the boys' parents.

Michel Tournier's book is quite an extraordinary achievement of transference, what I would call de-regionalisation and de-nationalisation, though, of course, it is one that is not at all unknown among the work of the English novelists of our own imperial period—a period which was a tremendous challenge to a man of imagination. I am thinking particularly of Kipling's short stories and novels about the Indian army; or of Henriques' writing about his experiences in the Sudan Defence Force; or of George Orwell's experience in the Burma police, as the beginning, really, of a bitter anti-colonial and anti-military evocation.

But Michel Tournier is almost unique, I think, in having used military service and having exploited defeat and national humiliation, collective humiliation, a deportation eastwards, and the very hard lottery of the defeated, to create for himself and for his hero, Tiffauges, a totally unfamiliar, yet oddly complete environment; all the more, of course, attractive, artistically at least, in that it is so fragile, is so dependent on the total fanaticism, the total commitment, of those very young boys: twelve, thirteen, fourteen, fifteen, all to be sacrificed; was indeed visibly cracking, as he rides around the frozen and dark countryside, in search of fair-haired boys. When they go to the military barber to have their heads shaved, he gathers up their soft blonde hair, to fill his pillows.

Le Roi des aulnes is indeed a regional novel, so firmly is it set in the lost borderlands of the Teutonic Knights. But it is also a novel of discovery and a novel of rejection. The discovery of a romantic Germany, irrational, primitive—even as the sound is heard of the Russian guns approaching steadily from the east, local archaeologists are at work, discovering and digging up the mummified bodies of early Teutonic settlers, preserved in the very marshy earth of this part of Europe. On the other hand, there is the rejection, not just of Paris and its suburbs: the previous experience of running a garage in Clichy-la-Garenne (again, the literary use of banality, comparable to that of Queneau); brushes with the French prison authorities, following an alleged *attentat à la pudeur* involving Martine, a sixteen-year-old *lycéenne*; but also a rejection of a provincial childhood and a Catholic boarding-school, a Catholic *internat* in Beauvais, in the course of which the main schoolfriend of Tiffauges succeeds in setting fire to the school.

Of course, one feels that Tournier's great novel *Le Roi des aulnes*, in its apocalyptic vision, represents, and is indeed meant to represent, the end of the road—and, one hopes, a road which Europe will never have to embark on again, with its fearful consequences. I suppose it is some minor compensation for the horrors of military collapse, defeat, and occupation that it is the defeated countries that generally seem to produce the most effective evocations of war, possibly because they are areas of military experience which reach down deeper and are more individual than successful operations.

The sort of military novels I have been discussing have, I think, reached their end, if only because, nowadays, young Frenchmen are offered such a wide range of choice: military service in a conventional form for a shorter period, or various forms of voluntary work, a lot of it, for example, educational or medical, over a longer period, so that a great many young Frenchmen would now opt for, say, educational service somewhere in North Africa or in one of the francophone African states, like the Côte d'Ivoire, Cameroun, or Senegal. These new opportunities have already produced a new topography of French literary experience, in the form of a number of very interesting novels about life, society, politics in recently independent francophone African states. Perhaps the most remarkable is a novel by Georges Conchon about what appears to be the Central African Republic, although the republic in question is never firmly located. So this is one possible prolongation, as it were, of the military novel.

The other general point I think one can make is that, in line with French military thinking, in terms of forms of defence against possible nuclear attack, there has been the formation of small units based on fairly small regional groupings; not one national army, but twenty regional armies, each composed of soldiers from a particular region—something which the whole military effort of the Third Republic did its best to eradicate, something that really goes back to the tradition of before the French Revolution, after which the regional names of the old royal regiments, for example, Royal Languedoc, were abolished, and cavalry or regiments of the line were given anonymous numbers.

What sort of effect this may have on military experience as expressed later, in twenty or thirty years' time, in the sort of literature I have been trying to describe and circumscribe, I do not know, but it is rather ironical, I think, that maybe this type of military thought may give an entirely new life to French regional literature as a whole, and not just regional literature in military terms. This is only a surmise, but I think it does offer some interesting possibilities for perhaps even the reinforcement of what I would describe as a very natural and very healthy cultural regionalism.

5

Blood and Soil

Any reference to *le roman régional*, whether in France or in some other French-speaking country, is likely, I think, to provoke something of a shudder of alarm at the prospect of long-winded and tiresome mediocrity; it often has the same sort of deadening effect, even, *au départ*, as what, in historical terms, can be described as *l'ouvriérisme*, a very useful form of research concerned with the history of the French working-class movement, and illustrated in such specialised reviews as *Le Mouvement Social*, and which, in English terms, can sometimes be described as Jack Crankshaft history—you know the sort of thing, the 1889 Penge lavatory attendants' strike.

At its very worst, *le roman régional* will either take the form of the grim and sordid *roman de la terre*, with its bestiality and incest; the *veillée*; the ancestors—great-grandfather, grandfather, grandmother—sitting by the hearth, recalling past disasters and ancient times, with references to terrible beasts, noises in the night, witches, the *bête du Gévaudan*, children nourished by wolves and the beasts of the field, the whole damned sort of French Walpurgis Night.

There is also the quite as intolerable 'up the skirt' type of peasant novel of the vintage proposed in the 1930s by Marcel Aymé's *La Jument verte*, about a village in the Franche-Comté. It is an extremely unfunny evocation of peasant lechery, though I must confess that I find it very difficult to be amused by this subject.

Then there is the Ancestral School—the gradual accumulation of the family heritage in land, each generation buying up this little parcel or that little bit of land so as to get *le lopin de terre arrondi*, something that the purchaser can pass on to the next generation; in fact, the whole idea of the peasant economy being a family economy, and not in the possession of even the oldest male member of that family. The younger brothers, if they wish to remain on the land, are probably depressed into the situation of being simply labourers for the oldest brother, the sisters probably go off to the towns in search of work in factories or in domestic service, and thus fall out altogether from the peasant society. It is the ennoblement of what I think of as rather sordid peasant acquisitiveness.

Accompanying it is the standard biography of this or that character—*fils de paysan, petit-fils de paysan, petit-fils de paysan champenois*—and then, behind him, *plusieurs générations formées dans le dur labour de la terre*—ancestral influences. There are also provincial influences that will somehow beckon the child on, even in a later urban existence, if uprooted from the soil, so that it is important for one's understanding of this person or that, even when removed from the rural community, that he or she, but particularly he (because these are very masculine concepts, it seems to me) is, let us say, *de vieille souche périgourdine, de vieille souche lyonnaise, forézienne*, or wherever, rather as if people were plants, with their roots growing in the soil, and as if their behaviour, even in a purely urban topography, were permanently conditioned by landscape, by the landscape of their place of birth, even if, after the first five or ten years of their existence, they left it.

The sort of thing that I have in mind comes either in the introduction or in the first chapter of this type of novel. It will start off with references to the shape of the countryside of the birthplace—to the *rudes contours du Lubéron*, or of Poitou, or to the *douces vallées de la haute Seine*, or of the Aude, or some other river. Very often, too, there will be references to the *sous-sol*—clay or chalk or basalt—as though this also had a direct moulding, as it were, on the future development of the main subject of such a novel. Then we move on to the actual physical description of the character or the other characters involved in this novel—*la figure taillée dans le granit*, and this sort of thing. It is rather as if, for instance, all Bretons had to be like that famous Parisian singer Fréhel, who took as her pseudonym the name of one of those jagged promontories at the end of the Breton peninsula, Cap Fréhel; so that all Bretons would have to have periwinkle-coloured eyes—*aux yeux pervenches*—as though a Breton could not have eyes of another colour.

In fact, the manner is what I would describe as *du faux paysan*. It can be found in the work of Charles Péguy, or of Barrès, especially in his novel *Les Déracinés*, meaning 'the uprooted ones'. Barrès' father was from the Pyrenees, as his surname indicates, and he is therefore only half a Lorrainer, a sort of *demi-Lorrain*; perhaps on account of this he became almost a professional Lorrainer, a male descendant of Jeanne d'Arc.

Roman régional equals *roman de la terre*, a late-nineteenth-century mode very much for the use of the townsman, and designed, perhaps unconsciously, to flatter the recently assimilated urban middle classes with the evidence of their material and, above all, I suppose, educational successes. One comes across such revealing phrases in this type of novel, or, indeed, very often in autobiography, as: '*Moi qui n'étais que fils de berger,*' '*Je me promenais en blouse et chaussé de sabots,*' '*Je faisais les quatre kilomètres, les pieds nus, pour aller à l'école communale.*' It provides an evocation of bucolic bliss and simplicity all the more agreeable for being savoured *en pantoufles* in a hideously furnished apartment, *faux Henri II*, or in a villa *faux manoir normand*, in La-Celle-Saint-Cloud, or in one of the *arrondissements* of Paris. In *La Terre*, Émile Zola, who knew his urban public, and particularly his Parisian public, discovered a goldmine. Even an ageing communist senator, like Jacques Duclos, in his memoirs, is liable to wax lyrical on the subject of his childhood as an apprentice baker—*un garçon boulanger*—in a very isolated village in the Hautes-Pyrénées: the tinkle of cowbells, long black stockings, a large hunk of coarse bread to take to the *école communale* to eat at lunchtime.

Generally speaking, peasants do not write books, but one feels that, if they did write about themselves, they would be much more likely to recall such unprecedented stages in their lives as, for example, service in the First World War, or anything, however horrible, however catastrophic, that took them out of the implacable round of agricultural work. Peasants, I think, would not regard their daily or their seasonal toil as worth writing about, so townsmen write about it for them—for other townsmen.

This is one aspect of the peasant novel, particularly at the turn into the present century. Another, and one which is possibly even more objectionable and, politically, certainly much more harmful, represents the nostalgic evocation of this or that province, or this or that *pays*, in the service of various brands of sub-nationalism.

Perhaps the most boring of the species would be the Flemish peasant novel, in the manner of Félix Timmermans, written in Flemish, and written as much to promote that language to literary respectability as to produce a work of literary imagination. A great deal of the work of Maxence van der Meersch, once he unwisely abandons the completely familiar urban triangle of Lille, Roubaix, and Tourcoing, and of the canal of Roubaix, teeters in this direction, with a great many hints of ancestral roots, references to the

sound of bells from Bruges belfries and *béguinages*, and references
to the waterlogged fields of West Flanders, its earth also soaked in
the blood of ancient and knightly battles; *Maria fille des Flandres*,
as if both Belgian provinces, East and West, and the French one to
boot, on the other side of the border, had somehow combined to
give birth to the tiresome girl who would not settle down to a
decent urban existence owing to the contradictory pulls of the triple
atavisms of a once-united Flanders.

Equally tiresome as literature and, ultimately, I think, as per-
nicious as nationalist propaganda, is the stodgy *summum* of novels
and children's stories about Alsace published in French between
1870 and 1914. First of all, the ineffable Hansi, from Colmar, who
illustrated his own books, a man who has a great deal to answer for
in bringing up perhaps two generations of French schoolchildren in
intense and almost visceral Germanophobia. Hansi's Germans are
always grotesque, the men always smoke squiggly pipes, wear
strange belted and buttoned jackets which have many pockets in
curious places, with a sort of plus-fours and heavy shoes; the
women always have corn-coloured hair, wear glasses, have long
teeth, and are most unfeminine.

One has the impression that no self-consciously regionalist
demonstration could ever have been complete during this period,
or, indeed, even after the recovery of the lost provinces, without the
presence of *l'Alsacienne maison*—her last manifestation, I suppose,
would be handing over the keys of a liberated Strasbourg to de Lat-
tre de Tassigny in 1944, once the town had been recovered for
French rule—and *l'Alsacien maison*, in his red waistcoat with silver
buttons. Daudet and Giono have often obliged with the same sort
of machine goods, for quite different areas of Provence; Henri
Queffélec, and others, for Brittany, whether of the Gallo- or of the
bretonnant variety. It is certainly no accident that there was an of-
ficially sponsored revival of this type of literature, part historical,
part folklore, under Vichy, particularly in the period 1940-42.

However, the regional novel does not necessarily have to be any
of these things; it does not even have to be rural. It can just as well
be accommodated to an urban setting. But it does have to belong to
a given period of French history, albeit a long one. It was a period
of relative social immobility, a period in which, in administrative
terms, the *département*, the *arrondissement*, and the *canton* were
very much basic units of political influence and manipulation, with
considerable over-representation of rural as opposed to urban

constituencies. It was a period during which small market and small administrative towns—*chefs-lieux d'arrondissement, sous-préfectures*—were grossly over-represented, and during which agricultural interests were greatly favoured, and in which political influence still went very often with land; hence the importance, in political terms, of the veterinary surgeon, the country doctor, the apothecary, as ideal small-town and rural electoral agents. And there was the agricultural economic lobby: the beetroot producers—the *betteraviers*; the wine *over*producers from the industrial wine regions—the *département* of the Hérault, the Algerian *départements*, parts of the Haute-Garonne; the market-gardening influences and so on in the neighbourhood of Paris, in the Seine-et-Oise. The regional novel, like these lobbies, is, I think, as good a representation of the relative changelessness of the Third Republic as any other.

In the heyday of the Third Republic, the deputy and even more the senator—generally a man of considerable girth, as if representing agricultural interests in his sheer size, and a man nearly always bearded—were important men, the makers and the breakers of countless ministries. Had such people been able to take off more time from the daily grind of what historians and political theorists have described as *la politique du bureau de tabac*, that is to say, the daily effort to keep up with the incoming mail from devoted parents asking, 'Can you get my son into the Paris police?' or 'Can you get me fixed up with the state monopoly?'—hence the term *la politique du bureau de tabac*—many deputies, I suppose, would no doubt have made quite admirable local novelists, so well had they got to know their various regional fiefs; and as a great deal of French literature has always been about politics, much of the literature of the Third Republic has been about regional politics.

The popularity, indeed, of the regional novel might possibly be related, particularly under the Third Republic, to the popularity, and indeed great influence, of *la presse régionale*. Certainly, for instance, a prewar reader of *L'Ouest-Eclair*, a newspaper which dominated the whole of the Breton peninsula and the Atlantic *départements* of France, would have been drawn to René Bazin as a writer from the west writing about the west. And most regional newspapers, at least from the 1880s onwards, would also publish a daily or weekly section in the local dialect, in the local patois, giving somewhat ponderous examples of local humour. For instance, 'Le Coin du Bruteux' in *La Croix du Nord* or *Nord Éclair*, both newspapers aimed primarily at the readership of the triple towns of Lille, Roubaix, Tourcoing. There was 'La Chronique de Gnafron' in Le Progrès—Gnafron being the Mr. Punch figure in the guignol lyonnais, the people's philosopher and sage who spends much of his time beating with a stick the gendarme or some interfering woman. Others included 'Les Propos de César', in Le Provençal, and 'Le Père Magloire', dressed up in the blues of a Normandy peasant and with his traditional peaked cap, in the old Journal de Rouen.

Perhaps such populist literature can never be very great literature, but, for a historian at least, it carries particular conviction, both as a témoignage, and as endowing the reader with a comforting sense of triumph, of penetration, as though he has broken a code, or discovered a password to gain admission to the closely guarded speech of the criminal underworld of the tapis-francs of the Île de la Cité, in Les Mystères de Paris and in other nineteenth- and twentieth-century populist literature on the subject of Parisian crime. We can no more dispense with the patois of great cities than we can dispense with rhyming slang, or with the inverted, but ingenious, slang of professional crime.

But we should not take the analogy between the regional novel and the press, carefully tailored to the interests and information of a restricted readership, too far. Certainly, as a period piece and as a point in French history, the regional novel naturally coincides with the proliferation of local sociétés savantes, concentration on local history, though local history seen in national terms, and rather as an accurate mirror, to scale, of national events, and, indeed, the local supremacy of the deputy, the senator, and, above all, the député-maire, the best possible combination. Thus, Gabriel Chevallier's famous novel Clochemerle (the town is easily identifiable as La Clayette, a town of about 3000 inhabitants—a chef-lieu d'arrondissement—in the Saône-et-Loire, with an anti-clerical municipality) was one of the great commercial successes of the period immediately before the Second World War. I think one of the reasons for its immense popularity was just that it was so reassuringly local, as, for instance, completely to exclude Hitler, and other equally alarming shadows beyond the frontiers of a healthily banal republic. Clochemerle could only belong to this particular and, as it turned out, final stage of the horse-dealing politics—the maquignonnage—of the Third Republic: a political satire on the well-worn theme of the pissotière, characteristic of a

certain republican irreverence—anti-parliamentary, gently mock-
ing the system of rewards and favours, but certainly not calling
it into question.

Even if rural France underwent, in the 1930s, as we are told by
Gordon Wright and other agricultural historians, the very begin-
nings of a peasant revolution, and even though many of the *départements* of the Massif Central were already feeling the effects of
depopulation, the values of a peasant smallholder and an artisan
society were still largely unquestioned. Thus, in the immediate
postwar period, the general reader, even the Parisian, could at once
identify with the stylised characters of *Clochemerle*—comic figures,
figures as caricatural as a pack of joke cards, as reassuringly immutable as Homais or the figures of Happy Families.

6
L'Exode and After

Though the events of the summer of 1940 totally destroyed the small-town, and rather miniature, politics of the Third Republic, as well as the régime itself, it did, on the other hand, give a new, completely original, and totally unexpected dimension to literary regionalism and, indeed, to a fresh discovery of the sheer diversity of France, the very wealth and variety of which might have appeared as a sort of comforting compensation for the dreadful shock of national humiliation—the total military collapse and utter defeat.

For one thing, *l'Exode*, that vast movement of population, was a marvellous inspiration to every type of literary exploration and discovery. It was a sort of fully fledged picaresque novel, and one lived out by up to ten million people. Hordes of civilians—refugees, deserters, convicts, lunatics—set off south-westwards, in the general direction of Bordeaux, Toulouse, Montauban, Mazamet, Tulle, Rodez, Perpignan, Vichy itself, Lyons, Marseilles, and Nice. There was simply no telling where people might end up, when they had stopped rolling. Once arrived at a destination, one which was often the result simply of luck or chance—the discovery of an empty room, or the discovery of an available bed—they would be likely to stay put for the next two or three years. Georges Simenon and large groups of other Belgian refugees found themselves finally washed ashore in the two Charentes, or in the Lot or the Gers. Parisian intellectuals discovered Toulouse or took stock of their bearings in Lyons. Parisian poets, actors, hangers-on of the Jockey Club, together with a ragged crowd of refugee anti-Nazis and socialist politicians, came across one another, again and again, wandering bewilderedly in the sun, up and down La Canebière, the famous street in Marseilles. Such accidents often lent to the national experience of total collective collapse an agreeable holiday experience of sun and shadow—the dark greens of the Midi and the unmistakable smell of the tideless Mediterranean.

The novelist Francis Ambrière wrote of those strange occupation years as *Les Grandes Vacances*—the title of his autobiographical novel—and the analogy is, I think, entirely appropriate. Henri Queffélec, a Breton writer, was able to investigate the molecular structure of the *bourgeoisie marseillaise* for his semi-autobiographical novel about Marseilles between 1940 and 1942 called *Le Journal d'un salaud*, while young Emmanuel Le Roy Ladurie, a *bas Normand* from Falaise, and, I suppose, aged about eleven in 1940, was, as a result of his father's promotion to a ministerial post in Vichy, exposed to the completely unfamiliar climate and mores of Montpellier.

Such a gigantic and unprecedented series of shifts in the temporary distribution of population, while certainly not conducive, in any way, to a sense of national solidarity in shared adversity, was, inevitably, greatly enriching, in terms of literary creation.

The immediate effect of *l'Exode* was, quite understandably, I suppose, to divide the population of France into two mutually antagonistic groups: refugees, when they stopped moving; and locals, who had never moved. The Parisians, as always, were almost universally unpopular. The Marseillais eyed askance the armies of northerners who placed a further burden on diminishing food supplies. Yet relative acclimatisation did ensue, especially once many of the northerners began to resign themselves to the fact that an early return to Paris, or to the Nord, or to the Pas-de-Calais, or, indeed, to Belgium, was out of the question. Furthermore, however unpleasant the initial experience—the terrible conditions on the roads; the shock of exile; the scattering of families; and the realisation, which would often come as a great shock, that one could be a total stranger in one's own country—*l'Exode* took the form of a voyage of discovery *à l'intérieur*, of a wealth and a freshness that no travel agency could possibly have achieved. For children, especially, the hazards of living for months out of suitcases contained elements of a game of adventure to be recalled nostalgically years later.

So there is a literature of *l'Exode* which has something of the spice and excitement of an eighteenth-century picaresque novel. Indeed, I think the analogy of the eighteenth century is altogether appropriate to a situation in which several million people, as a result of the total breakdown of public and private transport, were forced to walk. Many people could thus rediscover, or perhaps discover for the very first time in their lives, the slow pace of exploration as a changing landscape unwound itself to the painfully forward progress of a pedestrian overburdened with a battered suitcase in each hand, and probably a heavy rucksack on his or her back. To walk into a town, first through its suburbs, past squat, low-lying factories, with long ochre walls, spelling out, at immense length, the *défense d'afficher*; then past railway yards, goods yards; then through residential quarters; then, finally, to encounter the shopping centre, the cathedral, and the usual administrative accoutrements—*sous-préfecture, Banque de France, commissariat de police, contributions directes, contributions indirectes, lycée de filles, lycée de garçons*—is to discover that town afresh, and to recapture a true sense of distance and of the relationship, in human terms, of one quarter to another, and of the whole to the surrounding and enveloping countryside.

A walk through the June, July, and August of that fantastic, limpid, derisively beautiful summer of 1940 would expose the pedestrian to a mounting awareness of changes in domestic and in village architecture, in the shape of church towers and church spires, in landscape, and even in the seasons, for, by the time many people had actually stopped walking, the trees would have started to turn, even in the south, and, in Marseilles, the bitter mistral, the cold north-east wind that blows from the Alps down the Rhône Valley, would have given the Parisian a foretaste of the rigours of a winter in that windy, creaking city. And the winters of occupation and privation were like no other winters before or since: fireless rooms, huddling in heatless trains, riding on rickety bicycles. And in their search for eggs, butter, potatoes, rabbits, and poultry, the professional man and the city woman were offered, perhaps for the first time, direct and surprised contact with the often disagreeable realities of a hard, tight-fisted peasant society. Food shortage, which was especially acute in the Massif Central and in the Midi, particularly in the coastal strips of Provence, rationing, the development of a series of black markets and other *marchés parallèles*, produced (perhaps a peripheral benefit) both a rediscovery of a neglected and largely ignored peasantry and the revival of the novel about rural life, in the entirely new form of B.O.F.—*beurre, oeufs, fromage*—one of a series of new initials to have sprung into public awareness and, indeed, into the French vocabulary during that peculiar period. Food thus became a constant and haunting theme of novels concerned with the occupation and with the immediate post-occupation years, giving us, among others, *Au Bon Beurre*, by Jean Dutourd; *Le Vin de Paris*, by Marcel Aymé; *La Bête Mahousse*, by Jacques Perret; *La Truite*, by

Roger Vailland; and *Le Journal d'un salaud*, by Henri Queffélec.

Closely related to this new awareness of regional diversity is the extraordinarily enriching and varied experience of the Resistance, another unprecedented activity for which there was no proper training, and which imposed upon the urban intellectual and city-dweller regular and often intimate contact both with the country*man* and with the country*side*, the *résistant* needing the skills of the former, and the nooks, folds, and fastnesses of the latter. Resistance of course often took urban forms, acquainting Parisians with the peculiar geography of Lyons and its suburbs, with Marseilles and its *corniches* and not so distant discreet *calanques*; but it could not have survived at all without its semi-permanent rural pockets. Furthermore, save with the *cheminots*—by definition a national body—all forms of Resistance were forced to make do with limited regional areas, the limitations being imposed above all by the inward-looking guarantees to security provided by a narrow network of neighbourliness, friendship, acquaintanceship, trust, and, indeed, perhaps even more important, mistrust; for it was only in the countryside that the fact that a young man worked for *la Milice* would be universally known. At its most, a *réseau* might embrace a Department: *le réseau de l'Ain*, Georges Guingouin in the Haute-Vienne, *le réseau du Jura*, some of the Breton groups; but it would generally be confined to a more intimate geography, manageable on foot or by bicycle.

Even Kessel's *L'Armée des ombres*, a novel claiming to a national scale, is largely situated first in and around Marseilles, then in Lyons, both entirely recognisable in his descriptive topography; Vailland's *maquisards* stick to the rolling hills and lakes of the neighbourhood of Lons-le-Saulnier; Jacques Perret never strays from the Ain; and the considerable literature devoted to the *affaire Hardy*, at once polemical, political, and creative—for it *is* a marvellous story of human frailty, courage, and doubt, is firmly located in Lyons,[1] in la Croix-Rousse, and its north-eastern exit at Caluire. Other Resistance novels are centred on Annemasse and the vital border between France and Switzerland; others again

---

[1] On 21 June 1943, the newly formed Conseil National de la Résistance met in a doctor's house in the Lyons suburb of Caluire. It was a full meeting that included Jean Moulin, *le général* Delestraint, and the engineer René Hardy. The German authorities had obtained information about the time and place of the meeting, and surrounded the house, which had no exit from the back. All those attending were arrested, and subsequently tortured and killed, with the exception of Hardy, who, though wounded, managed to escape. He had been arrested by the Gestapo some time previously, but had parted company with his captors by jumping off a train. It

evoke another, bizarre, and fortunately evanescent frontier, within France itself, at such places as La Charité, Moulins, Orthez, previously dormant provincial towns of reassuring obscurity, and now all at once the gateway to hope or to disaster. The *résistants*, as they dragged their massive suitcases, holding transmitters, clandestine propaganda, or weapons, down country lanes, like the townsman in search of food, journeyed deep into the *plat pays*, acquiring in the process a unique and not to be repeated knowledge of isolated hamlets and of places well away from the dangerous R.N.

Collaboration, too, as well as having its literature, possessed its *hauts lieux*, its points of sociability and contact, and its torture-palaces. Vichy, above all, cries out for its novelist, although it has been extremely well served in recollections and memoirs. A capital with its ministries in hotel bedrooms, and its armies of secretaries working in hotel bathrooms, its table-talk under the heavy candelabra of the extraordinarily ornate dining-room of the Hôtel du Parc, calls out for even more comic and even less wide-eyed treatment than in René Benjamin's extraordinary propaganda piece written in 1942, *Dans les Pas du Maréchal*, which has such gems of observation as, for instance, '*Quand le maréchal [Pétain] marche, il prend possession du trottoir, mettant un pied devant l'autre.*' And also gems of the ancient Marshal's table-talk: '*Bouthillier, parle-moi des Chinois. Ils sont jaunes, n'est-ce pas? Je n'aime pas les jaunes.*' Think of the opportunities to a novelist of a situation in which the capital of a great European country suddenly finds itself in the French equivalent of, let us say, Harrogate, or Malvern, or Llandrindod Wells.

In Paris, the *fine fleur* of collaboration stuck prudently to the *beaux quartiers*, the *VIIIme*, *XVIme*, and *XVIIme arrondissements*, just as the Germans themselves showed a marked preference for the avenue du Bois, the avenue Foch, the rue de Rivoli, and the avenue de l'Opéra. The strange and silent city depicted in that extraordinary film of 1944, Bresson's film *Les Dames du Bois de Boulogne*, and the equally strange and silent city of the sickly novelist Drieu la Rochelle, the author of *Gilles*, is confined to the *XVIme arrondissement*, to the avenue Henri-Martin—and to

was later argued by some leading *résistants* that the Germans had let him escape and had used him to lead them to the secret rendezvous in Caluire. Hardy was subsequently tried. There has been an abundant literature on the subject of his guilt or innocence, including books by Hardy himself. The *affaire Hardy* is likely to remain one of the many unsolved mysteries of *la clandestinité*.

the *VIIIme*. Only the other ranks, German soldiers on leave, were likely to be let loose in the pleasure spots of Pigalle and the Place Blanche, in the *IXme arrondissement*. It is doubtful, I think, if the occupiers would have been seen at all in the *XVIIIme*, *XIXme*, and *XXme*, or in the *XIIme*, the more working-class *arrondissements* of north-eastern and eastern Paris. From the experience there has grown up a sinister geography of evocative street-names: la rue Lauriston, la rue Lesueur, the blue and white plaques of which still send a slight shudder down the backs of passers-by of my generation.

There are other peculiarities of Occupied Paris that have been touched upon by novelists like Marcel Aymé, particularly in that marvellous book of short stories published under the general title of *Le Vin de Paris*, which is the title of one of the stories, and by people who have written their memoirs of this period—people like Jean Galtier-Boissière and Emmanuel d'Astier de la Vigerie. All note the strange silence, the emptiness, and the cleanliness of the city; also the absence of dogs and traffic, except for those strange *vélo-taxis*—almost like baskets; they could take two people and were drawn by athletic cyclists. The Métro, though crowded beyond belief, was still operating on all its lines, while the highly dangerous frontiers of railway stations, particularly termini, were an ambience of stillness and waiting, of hidden menace and impending violence. But with a disarmingly reassuring everydayness, children were still pouring in and out of *lycées*, perhaps only vaguely aware of the absence of their Jewish *condisciples*. The café terraces were crowded with French civilians and German soldiers, sometimes side by side. The titles of the newspapers, *Le Matin*, *Le Journal*, *L'Écho de Paris*, *Le Petit Parisien*, and *L'Oeuvre*, were the same as before the war, but with very different contents.

An ancient *réseau métropolitain*, already forty or fifty years old, ground along on its fixed subterranean, or semi-subterranean, or, indeed, overhead *itinéraires*, still to the sight of the advertisement 'Dubo . . . Dubon . . . Dubonnet', the flickering icons of a now discredited and rejected Third Republic. In fact, the Occupation is a whole area of national and individual experience that, mercifully, no doubt, has been denied to English letters.

Perhaps in fact we are better at *ambience*, at landscape, than the French, who seem so often hardly to use their eyes and who put in scenery, almost as an afterthought, as a backdrop to a human situation, to a story, to *l'intrigue*. No French novelist really succeeds

in depicting the *physical* reality of wartime Lyons or Marseilles
(the latter best described, in fact, by Victor Serge, in one of his
political novels), and even the most poetical and hauntingly
beautiful novel of all Occupation literature, Vercors' *Le Silence de
la mer*, while firmly set in time, class, and *colloque*, floats foggily in
a conventional park surrounding a conventional *château*.

Exile, on the other hand, by sharpening an enveloping *mal du
pays*, has likewise produced a strongly evocative literature recalling
places and paradises temporally lost. French circles in London
during the war developed a literature of nostalgia that was at times
extremely powerful. I recall an astonishing description of the
sounds and smells of a Parisian working day, the first faint
rumbling of the Métro, and the unique odour of that surrealist
underground railway, in the monthly review *La France libre*. The
war, service in de Gaulle's forces, added a new, unexpected dimension to the military novel, taking its brave, but modest heroes to the
huge, desolate airfields of East Anglia, or offering brief respite from
savagery, danger, and death, the bitter-sweet masculine fraternity
of arms, in the love-affair of a convalescent French officer in Juin's
army with a Neapolitan lady, love being always the surest, most
potent, and most fragile form of escape from collective orthodoxies
and from the terrible world of courage and cowardice. Both Jules
Roy and Emmanuel Roblès have succeeded in portraying the brave
without sentimentalism, but with pity and dignity. Emmanuel
d'Astier de la Vigerie, a novelist and a *poète manqué* much more
than a politician, after describing the silent, beautiful, and empty
Paris of *juin '40*, moves on to Lyons and Marseilles, then to London and the Byzantine conflicts of Algiers, Carlton Gardens, the
French quarrelling like mad in exile, and observes, with French eyes
and with a mixture of astonishment and admiration, the Londoners
under the blitz. An experience so completely unusual as to bring
disparate groups of Frenchmen, of every political affiliation, and of
extremely varied social origins—adventurers, heroes, crooks,
royalists, Croix-de-Feu, aristocrats, monks, Protestants, in-
dustrialists, *Français du Brésil*, French Basques from Montevideo,
Gapançais from Argentina, French-speaking Mauritians with
splendid seventeenth-century surnames *à particule*, Bretons,
Parisians, *chtimis*, southerners, engineers, academics, actors,
garagistes, *châtelains*—to South Kensington, Bush House, and
Carlton Gardens, could not fail to produce a literature evocative of
the *realities* of London, not the fog-bound imaginings of MacOrlan

and Céline. The politics of exile and the years of lonely hope and courage undoubtedly made many participants and combatants, previously devoid of literary ambitions, into novelists of these new and bizarre dimensions, thus revealing a Romain Gary, a Jules Roy, a Kessel, and a Fourcade (*L'Arche de Noë*, though in fact a straightforward account of one of the earliest and longest-living Resistance groups, *reads* like a novel, rich in compassion, in picaresque episodes, and constantly threatened by danger, torture, and slow death).

The Liberation and its literary aftermath, mostly in the form of evocations of Resistance and collaboration, memoirs and novels recalling food shortage, black-marketeering, memoirs and novels about growing up in the peculiar circumstances of the Occupation years, represents, I think, the end of the regional novel, though, now and again, there have been revivals, such as the tender, bitter-sweet, and menacing description of the small port of Blaye, and the estuary of the Gironde, in Marguerite Duras' novel, *Moderato Cantabile*, which was made into a film. The definitive end of the regionalism of recognisably human proportions came with the end of the Fourth Republic, in 1958, and the imposition, from above, of vast economic and social units, devoid of human proportions and of an identifiable historical past. Saône-et-Rhône, l'Étang de Berre, the Port-Jérôme, and suchlike, represent the blueprints of technocrats, the District de Paris was much too vast to produce a literature of describable frontiers. The many new towns of the lower Seine Valley, of the Fos-Berre complex, the Part-Dieu outside Lyons, have so far remained unrecorded.

Of course, novelists will go on writing about their childhood, so that the regional novel is certainly assured of a few more years. And, indeed, five years ago, there was a most reassuring example of its still healthy condition in Ajar, in his novel of the childhood of an illegitimate child, an Arab brought up by a retired Jewish prostitute, Madame Rosa, in Belleville, in north-eastern Paris.[1] But what is one to make of the childhood of those who have grown up in the new towns, in Alphaville?

[1] *La Vie devant soi* (1974).

PART TWO

7

Queneau's Itineraries

The attraction, at least to a certain type of social historian, of much populist literature is that it is concerned with unpretentious people caught in a fixed, predictable pattern of habit, within the narrow frontiers of a topography that is especially reassuring in its banality and in its eminently human dimensions. The characters in such populist novels represent the very antithesis of Michel Tournier's Tiffauges; for they seldom put even a timid foot beyond the modest itineraries imposed by weekday work and leisure and by the limited, and generally unenterprising, excursions of the week-end. Of course, every now and then, public history will invade the timidly protected territory of private history, imposing, all at once, new, unprecedented, and extensive itineraries, such as those of *l'Exode*, of Resistance, and of *la France Libre*. But, sooner or later, barring such a gigantic catastrophe as that offered by a Revolution, or by a revolutionary situation—and the peaceable historian, from the safety of an eighteenth-century archive, will seek, in the exploration of the habitual, the readily acceptable, the repeatable, and the banal, the ultimate protection against such terrors as the sudden invasion of collective fanaticisms, their flying columns of unquestioning orthodoxy provided by groups of young vigilantes, and its reality—indeed the reality of *any* Revolution—illustrated by the presence of many corpses in many streets, soon objects almost as familiar as the happily domestic contents of shop-windows—habitual itineraries will once more offer the longed-for guarantee that one day will be much like the last, that Thursday will follow Wednesday, and that the week-end will conclude the week.

Within the different areas of their choice, Eugène Dabit, Hervé Bazin, René Fallet, Maxence van der Meersch, Marc Bernard, and even Henri Queffélec are all illustrators of habit, indeed of everydayness; and it is in their everydayness that we can so often recognise ourselves, exclaiming, as if suddenly catching sight of

oneself in a long mirror, set in one of the closed passages of the central *arrondissements* of Paris: 'that is exactly right,' or 'we have
been this way before' (and, as if to emphasise that everything is as it
should be, that is, as it was the day before, or the week before, a
brief pause, in front of one such freely offered mirror, perhaps on
the corner of a *boulangerie*, of a hatter's, or of an optician, to take
in one's own unimpressive features and regular appearance; during
the terrible panic of pre-Munich, I was in the habit thus of
reassuring myself as to my own existence and durability, in the
mirror of a *pâtisserie viennoise*, in the narrow part of the rue de
l'École de Médecine, and what I saw was so engagingly and
irretrievably civilian, unheroic, and ordinary, that I went away a
little bit happier; and throughout the Munich crisis and that of the
following year, the mirror represented a small shrine of self-
recognition: '*Bonjour, alors tu es encore là,*' just as, in other
periods, I would take similar precautions, in one of the many
mirrors of the Galeries Saint-Hubert, in Brussels, even when in
uniform, a uniform that in the sheer patina of dirt and constant
wear, eventually seemed to clothe me in an individuality of prudent
otherness, I was so untidy I hardly looked like any other soldier).
Such literature must be the very contrary of the picaresque, if only
because one has to take the same route, morning and evening, in
order to check up on the mirror; but also because the itineraries are
dictated by a combination of timidity, habit, the distance one is
prepared to walk, the desire to pass beneath the protective presence
of a stylised Étienne Marcel, or to look up at the gentle contours of
an eighteenth-century female Virtue—Modesty, Humility—leaning
invitingly on her plinth and smiling down into the street, or to see
whether a familiar wig is still slightly askew on the bald wooden
head in the window of a *coïffeur de dames*, and the existence of a
network of public transport above or below ground. To follow
exactly the same route each day, crossing from one pavement to
another at the same level, is a weapon in a personal armoury of
sameness and continuity, as if, from sheer familiarity, one could
deny such private and cosy itineraries to the red tidal waves of
Revolution as they rush down wide boulevards, or to the marching
of victorious armies down prestigious avenues. Thus, in Queneau's
book *Pierrot mon ami*, his prudent hero checks up, twice a day, on
the way in and on the way out, on the perpetual ballet of the jumping ball-bearings, *les roulements à bille 'Skif'*, in the windows of a
Swedish firm, avenue de la Grande Armée. Pierrot notes with

satisfaction that they dance, day and night, through the '30s, as indeed they continued to dance right through Occupation, Liberation, various Republics, and several attempted putsches, as a glorious affirmation of Swedish neutrality. And young René Fallet, on his Vespa, heading for Paris by the pont de Charenton, has his eyes open for similar signals, recognisable only to himself. And so, I suppose, might an inhabitant of Berlin, in April 1945, derive some exiguous promise from the familiar sight of a milk-cart, on its rounds, early in the morning, or even of a queue consisting of recognisable people.

It is not a geography to attract Céline, who can derive no satisfaction from the mirrored image of his tormented face, and who, as a writer, on the contrary, thrives on catastrophe and finds inspiration (like Lucien Rebatet in military collapse, in *Les Décombres*) for *D'un Château l'autre*, in the tumultuous train journey that, in the death throes of the Third Reich, took him, his wife, and the cat Bébert, from Sigmaringen to Copenhagen. The pounding wheels of night trains, as they move relentlessly eastwards, are the suitable orchestration to the certainty of catastrophe and death, so that it is appropriate that great steel trains, still in their peacetime colours, their out-of-date advertisements referring to civilian products, their photographs depicting lost holidays, should figure so emblematically in the war novels of Heinrich Böll and in the revolutionary poems of Cendrars. For these are convoys of death. Céline seeks out catastrophe, even travels far, by sea and by land, to reach it, as if in search of a distant earthquake zone, because he rejects bourgeois values, is a hater of mankind, and exults in general disaster. A similar exultation in violence is discoverable in Cendrars' attitude to the Russian Revolution, appreciated almost as an artistic, poetic experience; but unlike Céline, Cendrars, in pauses in between such excitements, likes to come down to rest, enjoying his regular *points de chute* and returning, again and again, to quiet and shady refuges, generally not too far removed from the Vieux Port, in Marseilles.

But, of all such populists, of all such novelists of urban (and suburban) itineraries, of all such poets of habit and banality, of all such prudent explorers of a narrowly circumscribed visible world of urban reassurance, the most endearing is undoubtedly Raymond Queneau. Queneau was a great many other things as well: a philosopher, a grammarian, a mathematician, a poet, a stylist, a magician of words and of accents, constantly experimenting in order to capture the exact cadence of Parisian speech (another form of populism). But it is as the unassuming pedestrian of a fixed circuit, as the regular user of *les transports communs*, the habitué of places where there are other habitués, and, above all, the novelist of le Havre and of certain peripheral areas of Paris that I appreciate him most. He is the ideal witness of the *little* in everything, of small dimensions and of a Hulot-proportioned urban or suburban architecture of a couple of storeys, or, at most, of three (not for Queneau, one feels, the tall narrow building of *Le Jour se lève*, an architecture of menace and blood). Queneau is both the poet of fixed itineraries—and some of his most attractive poems are written about the various lines—Nord-Sud and so on—of the Paris Métro—of the modest, even minuscule, and of the engagingly everyday; he displays a prodigious verbal talent to describe the smell of overflowing dustbins and of stuffy *loges de concierge*, he moves about on the frontiers of cities, on the edge of cemeteries, beside gasworks, opposite slaughterhouses, small soap-factories, and distilleries, his characters flee the grandiose (they only attend *l'Expo '37* in order to enjoy the amusement arcades, giving the vast exhibition-halls of Stalin's Soviet Union and Hitler's Germany not even a glance), fulfilling themselves in a landscape that is provincial in its modest proportions: *petit* restaurant, *petit* café, *petite gare*, *petit parc*, *petit square*, *petite province*, *petites gens*. Perhaps no one could be more provincial than an Havrais—Queneau would argue so—save, perhaps, an inhabitant of Clichy-la-Garenne or Rueil-Malmaison; for Paris and its suburbs provide a wonderful range of provinciality.

His is nearly always an urban topography *à petite échelle*, and so set to a scale that is human, individualistic, habitual, and, within manageable limits, eccentric. The poet in *Loin de Rueil*, whose fame extends even as far as Colombes and le Vésinet, possibly even to Suresnes and Puteaux, is modestly eccentric, in a proportion entirely reassuring to the limited expectations of his regular circle of admirers, listeners, and friends. Like a small statue on a provincial square—that, for instance, of *l'abbé* Barthélémy, the author of *Le Voyage du Jeune Anacharsis* (and that the locals refer to as *Le Jeune Anarchiste*), the pride of Pagnol's native Aubagne—like a bearded (*en éventail*), floppy-hatted, loose-tied poet, cut off half-way down, and his top half administered to by whole drooping Muses, who fan him with palm-leaves (perhaps indeed *les palmes* ?), shading in a concrete grotto in the formal garden of a *sous-préfecture*—like the bewigged Jacquart and his Machine, standing, impassible, like a schoolmaster among the pigmies of a Third Form, above the heads of those attending the weekly market in the main square of la Croix Rousse (Jacquart looks stonily towards Lyons, no one looks at him)—the Poet gives Rueil a measured ration of fantasy. He is a *poète de banlieue*, as much an object of pride within a small community as the Douanier at his Sunday-painting, or *le facteur* Cheval, adding to his Gothic Ruins; and so he will not overstep the mark set by prudent reverence, will not all at once take off on great Hugolien eagle's wings, but will stay, an object of honour to his restricted parish. If he has not been already, he too will eventually be rewarded with *les palmes académiques*, an award that will be noted in the local newspaper, and that will be celebrated around the *comptoir à zinc* of a *café-tabac* not far from the station, *ligne Saint-Lazare*. The *palmes* honour the small community and they represent the best guarantee that things are much as they used to be and that suburbanites can sleep tight behind their closed metal shutters, opening on to china storks, cats, and swans, onto garden gnomes, tiny coloured *châteaux-forts*, and patterns formed by scallop-shells, indicating a steady diet of *coquilles Saint-Jacques* and the débris of several years of Sunday *agapes*.

Such is the range of his interests and his themes, Queneau is a novelist and a poet, a humorist and a philosopher who is likely to have a very varied appeal to people of different, even opposing, tastes. There is, for instance, a romantic, 'Celtic Twilight' Queneau who writes of a totally imaginary Hibernia; and closest to this improbable disguise is that adopted by a writer embarking on a journey of fairy-tale and myth, full of hidden allusions that will escape the pedestrian of routinal itineraries who hits this boulevard or that, *à heure fixe*. *Exercices de style* can be taken both as an elaborate trapeze-act in comparative linguistics, or as a marvellously fresh, and constantly renewed, piece of social observation and aural testimony. The philosopher and the linguist will opt for the former interpretation, the historian will savour and admire the latter; both will no doubt be right. Equally, Queneau's childlike innocence, a quality that makes him one of the most delightful novelists of childhood and children—in a category that would put him with Marc Bernard and Pagnol—can easily lapse into quite gratuitous childish cruelty and violence that comes as a sudden jolt to a previous account of ordinariness and predictability. Queneau's sense of fun can become too strained, extending into a repetitively rumbustious fantasy and into an acceleration of incidents, as in a film run too fast, that so much detract from the value of *Zazie*. *A chacun son Queneau*; and this no doubt is how the author, who loved fooling people, would have liked it. For myself, he is a novelist of reassurance and habit, of a semi-private world that is apolitical, even outside politics, that attempts—often unsuccessfully—to shield itself from public events, and that is profoundly unrevolutionary. But, as I see him, he is also a novelist of period, most at home perhaps in the comforting banality of the 1930s and in a confined world in which there are hardly any echoes of Hitler, though the Front Populaire will obtrude as an insistent background to the complaints of *petits commerçants*, a sort of Greek chorus on the subject of the *assurances sociales*, endless strikes, and the likelihood that *l'Expo* will never open. One of his characters even chooses 1938 as a year in which to embark on a coach-tour of the Black Forest, and taking in Nuremberg as well. The threat of war is vaguely present, but to be brushed aside by conversation of such extreme banality as to include only the fate of neighbours, local gossip, and the weather. The private vocabulary is always more insistent than the public one, and, if one's livelihood consists of selling photograph-frames in silver or simili-silver, then it will be provided by breakneck sales talk. The 1930s are firmly present, at the level of the *faits divers* rather than of the Rhineland; and they are present too in the powerful element of cinema in all Queneau's novels. '*Faisons du cinéma*,' so many of his people seem to say; and off they go on journeys of fast-changing fantasy. But even Queneau's '40s succeed in bypassing the great disasters, thus suggesting that, despite them, habit can still survive. Even more, the alarming '50s can be tempered and tamed, to accommodate the irreverence and provinciality of *Zazie*. The language, however, remains very much that of the Parisian of the 1930s, just as much as the advertisements—and Queneau *loves* advertisements—are contemporaneous with the jingles of Radio-Paris on the subject of the Galeries Barbès and *les meubles signés Lévitan*. What no doubt offers a consistent thread through all three decades is the theme of *failure*. His characters are obsessed with the fear of failure, and indeed a great many do fail, landing with a most awful bump, just as one expected them to. One could see it coming. But sometimes it can be avoided. Most somehow manage just to keep going.

I have lived with Queneau for so long that I cling to him as to a lost friend; as long as he is around, things cannot be too bad. But he is no longer around; and his sudden death, in October 1976, deprived me of a long-awaited opportunity to visit him in Neuilly. I think I would have liked him as much as I liked what he wrote. I even think *he* would have liked my Zaharoff Lecture, which reached him two months before his death. He had a very nice face, round and designed for laughter, eyes that regarded the world with amusement, and a large round head as reassuring as that of a Norman shopkeeper.

I suppose the most surprising thing about Raymond Queneau was that he was so old when he died. He was born in February 1903; but it is very hard for me to think of him as an old man. There was something almost childlike about his humour, about his freshness; but there it is, he was one of a generation of French writers who really came into prominence in the early 1920s. I suppose one would associate him with Breton, with Apollinaire, Aragon as well; he was at one time regarded as a surrealist, insofar as one can ever say of Queneau that he ever belonged to any group. The novels come in fairly rapid succession right through the '30s and through the '40s. I suppose the last one, which is probably the best known in this country, partly because of the film, *Zazie dans le Métro*, is the only one of his novels that belongs to the '50s.

One can appreciate why the surrealists, at least early on, thought that Queneau was perhaps one of them; he has Aragon's eye for the sort of advertisements you would see in *les passages*—those closed passages that are so much part of Louis-Philippe's Paris—advertisements in public places like the Métro, in trains, in buses, or enormous things on the cut-off sides of houses that look as though they have been cut down like an ice-cream. He is very much influenced by things like the bizarre advertisements of the private detective agencies—'*Agence A—Z, filatures discrètes, discrétion garantie, divorces*'—and also the sort of advertisements that Queneau's world was subjected to, almost daily, through the newspapers. I remember one very well, one of those patent medicines that always had names which obviously fascinated Queneau because they were so ugly: '*Monsieur, c'est VOUS le coupable si Madame est frigide!*'—a picture of a nude lady sort of bending backwards in agony—and then '*Prenez du Fortifex,*' or something like that, and, you know, your troubles will be over and Madame will not be *frigide* any more. And for headaches—a picture of a bald man having a sort of croquet mallet being knocked into his head, and saying, '*Pour les maux de tête—Hypophigine*,' or something. Queneau is obviously fascinated by the inventiveness of these absolutely villainous pharmaceutical companies which take up so much of French advertising. It is very much part of the visual and verbal fantasy of Queneau and Queneau's *petites gens*, people who travel on the *transports communs*.

My own interest in Queneau started quite by accident when I was in Le Havre, and somebody there said, 'Well, if you're interested in Le Havre, you should read *Un Rude Hiver*,' one of the early Queneau novels; which I then did. It is always most exciting, I think, to read a regional novel *sur place*, because you are actually discovering the geography of the place at the same time as the author is illustrating it. The whole novel takes place during the most sinister part of the First World War, the terrible winter of 1916-17, with Le Havre one of the main base camps of the British forces—it is a novel based on his very close observation of life as a child between the ages of ten and thirteen or fourteen. He had a very good observation-point, his mother's shop in the Rue de Paris; his mother's *mercerie*, a general sort of haberdashery, was very much patronised by what you might call *la haute bourgeoisie havraise*.

I think that, with the passage of time, Queneau may have somewhat romanticised his mother's activities; I don't think her *mercerie* was a *petite mercerie*, the type of small general shop that recurs again and again in Queneau's subsequent novels about Paris. He has got a description of one with a few rather broken-down-looking tin soldiers in the window, a captain of the Zouaves waving his sword (and the sword has got bent), and a *garde républicain à cheval* (but he has lost his tall headgear), mixed up with papers, particularly *la presse enfantine*, *Les Pieds Nickelés*, the French equivalent of *Beano* and so on, hanging off clothes-pegs, along with one or two of the more popular *concierge*-type Parisian dailies—*Le Parisien Libéré*, *L'Aurore*—and some large bottles of rather flyblown-looking sweets.

This is one of his fixed points of observation for *la vie de quartier* in suburbs like Suresnes or Rueil. The other vantage-point which he used to great effect was the tram, in its fixed itineraries—first of all up and down the Boulevard Maritime, from the Bassin du Commerce, right along the front into the neighbouring semi-independent commune of Sainte-Adresse to the terminus in the point of the Cap de la Hève, where it climbs up—there's a cliff and a lighthouse—you've got there, all you can do is go back. Queneau would have been very aware of this sort of yoyo, this up-and-down tramline which would take him the whole of the front. He has a whole series of other points of observation at right angles to this one—the series of public transport tramlines that go inland. Le Havre is a very strange town. One generally thinks that areas on the heights overlooking a seaside town are going to be areas of well-to-do householders. In Le Havre, it wasn't so in Queneau's time, and as you come up to the heights, very steep up, almost clifflike, to places like Sanvic, Ingouville, and so on, you are then getting into very largely purely working-class areas.

Of course, any French provincial town on a Sunday takes on a certain quality of silence, punctuated early by church bells. And then figures, family groups *en grappe*, holding little rectangular boxes done up with gold string, from the *pâtisserie* which remains open on Sundays. They are going out to have lunch with *le cousin* or *la cousine, un tel, une telle,* and so on. Then for a time, from, say, half-past twelve until about three, the streets are silent and empty; and then slowly there emerge, walking sometimes with difficulty, battalions of family groups—*la promenade digestive*. In a place like Le Havre, *la digestion* will be more difficult because of *la cuisine à la crème, la cuisine normande*, helped down by a *coup de calvados*, so that the walk becomes more imperative. On the other hand, the choice of itineraries is almost inevitably limited to the sea-front—unless the weather's absolutely foul—the Boulevard Maritime, like an overpopulated fishing-ground, with large and small groups coming and going and greeting one another by *coups de chapeau*, rather like recognition signals from ships, protected more often than not by umbrellas, because Le Havre is a very wet place. It is an itinerary that is so reassuring as almost to make you scream; there is so little possibility of variety, unless the north-easter is howling so terribly you can hardly stand up. This is a peculiar quality of a seaside town which Queneau expresses very, very well, I think, in *Un Rude Hiver*.

This melancholy character, Bernard Lehameau—apart from going to the Front, which was the great adventure of his life, the war, mobilisation—what's he done? He has seen the split rock of Étretat on the Sunday excursion there and back, he has crossed over on the paddle-steamer from Le Havre to Honfleur, spent half an afternoon in Honfleur eating *moules*, and then taken the paddle-steamer back. He has been to Rouen once for some school outing, and that's it. And the lady who keeps the bookshop, who is the intellectual in *Un Rude Hiver*, the only one: she is always complaining about how brash and crass the Havrais are—all they think about is money and food and drink. She is regarded with an extreme mixture of contempt and disfavour because she is *basse-normande*—she comes from the other side of the river. In that sort of historical geography, it is the near neighbour you hate most.

The hero of *Un Rude Hiver* is a lieutenant in the French army who is on sick leave, a widower, who has had a very frustrated, unhappy existence. And what gradually unfolds is a very brief and rather tragic—nothing's ever *really* tragic in Queneau, but *rather* tragic, because so brief—love-affair, or *amitié amoureuse*, with a girl in the English services, the Women's Auxiliary Service. These two, gradually, very tentatively and very timidly, begin to discover one another—which is of course linguistically a marvellous opportunity for Queneau to convey what a Frenchman attempting to speak English sounds like, '*Zer Saouze Staffordshire Régiment*' and this sort of thing—'*you mai la-ouff, Miss Weeds*'—all of his necessarily very brief conversations with this girl, generally when he is having to shout, and she too, against the terrible noise of the wind, the sea, and the pebbles being ground up and down. This relationship is explored against the background of this very limited geography, either up and down the Boulevard Maritime, or inland from the *sémaphore*.

The next stage is that Miss Weeds is posted back home, and that is all very sad, and that is the end of that. He never hears from her again. One of the troop transports is torpedoed off Le Havre—she might have been on it, she might not, one doesn't know.

The rest of the novel is the hero's—Bernard Lehameau's —gradual discovery of a working-class family. One gathers (as one gathers most things in Queneau, peripherally), filtered through the two small children—a girl, I suppose about twelve, and her little brother, Polo, who is about nine—all the activities of the bread-winner of this family, orphaned family, 'our elder sister', '*not*' *grande soeur*', who is very pro-Allied. The little boy lets out in the tram one day that '*ah, not*' *grande soeur, elle parle très bien l'anglais;—elle ne parle que l'anglais toute la journée, toute la nuit.*' And his elder sister goes very red, and then it comes out that *not*' *grande soeur* is indeed extremely hospitable towards the Allied forces, particularly officers, and the children are so familiar with this, they know the cap-badges of nearly all the regiments, and they try

Bernard on the tram, they sort of test him out on it—'What is the cap-badge of the South Staffordshire?'

As one comes towards the climax of this exploration, as it were downwards, through love, of a different social milieu, Bernard goes and tells the old lady in the bookshop, 'I'm going to get married,' and she says 'Oh, a very good idea. I hope you're not marrying an Havraise.' 'Oh yes, I am, but *c'est une ouvrière*.' And then there's a last scene of him going up the hill in this squeaking, dragging tram as it climbs up and up towards Sanvic and Graville, up to the white villa where Madeleine receives her officer friends. The front room is full of their photographs and so on, it's a white villa with red *ardoises*, red tiles, and there is a small garden and white gates, and a china cat on the doorstep and a china dog in the sort of *pignon*, on the roof over the porch. It ends up as a very happy, a rather moving love story with an inconclusive ending—he's going to marry this girl, the younger sister, and you are left, as it were, *sur l'expectatif*, because he has been pronounced fit and will be going back to the Front.

Although the first novel of his I ever read is, of course, indelibly marked by outside events—that is to say by the Great War—one feels that Queneau himself is completely apolitical, that his characters are poor men's philosophers who say, 'Oh, the only thing worth reading in the paper is the crime column, *les guerres, les sports, enfin, la foutaise*'—people mostly living on something of a shoestring, changing jobs frequently. Hence the attraction both to Queneau and to his characters of the semi-fantasy world, of Luna-Park, the pleasure beach, the circus, and the dodgems.

The people he generally writes about are small independent artisans, shopkeepers, restaurant-owners, publicans, *cafetiers*, *vins-charbons*, *bougnats*, perhaps slightly eccentric small inventors, backyard inventors and people like that—*ferrailleurs*. It is exceedingly reassuring, the Queneau world, and will include the faithful group who will find themselves, first of all, for the *pousse-café*, in the Café de la Gare or whatever it is, every morning, and then again at *l'heure de l'apéritif*, and then again at the *restaurant des habitués*, each with his napkin ring and so on and so forth. It *is* reassuring, because you feel that it has got a sort of continuity of its own as long as you stick in it, as long as you do not imprudently put your foot out of it—across the river, go into another quarter. . . .

Monsieur Queneau once did me the great honour of sending me
a book of his poems about the Métro, and he signed it, '*À mon ami
Richard Cobb, Raymond Queneau—Havrais de Paris*', and this of
course is really how I like to see Queneau, as something rather out
of the ordinary in the very ancient tradition of the provincial *qui
bat le pavé Paris, les dangers de la ville*, and all that sort of thing. I
think it's very important when you're considering writers as well as
ordinary people, how did they come into the city? And the usual
points of entry, from the mid-nineteenth century onwards, for ambition, literary talent, judicial talent, and so on, would be the Gare
de Lyon or the Gare d'Austerlitz, the whole theme that you get in
the Daudet novels and so on of the ambitious young southerner, the
méridional, qui monte à Paris—and this is the theme of so many
political novels in nineteenth- and twentieth-century France, this is
the theme indeed of so many political careers, especially of the
Third Republic, which was so much dominated by southern
politicians. But in terms of French literature a talent that came from
upper Normandy, arrived in Paris Gare Saint-Lazare, and then ex-
ploits those areas of Paris which somehow still nestle on the Norman side, the downstream side of the city, is very rare—I think
Queneau would describe himself as a Norman writer. He is in some
ways unique in this respect, of somebody who *descend sur Paris*, '*ce
n'est pas monter—ça descend sur Paris*'; not *la montée à Paris*. And
in his subsequent novels he doesn't abandon this. He never turns his
back on Le Havre—in this novel or that novel things go from
catastrophe to catastrophe—divorce, threatened bankruptcy,
terrible blue letters from the Préfecture, and this sort of thing—how
do you react? '*Oh, si, on allait au Havre*'—and you take the train
from Saint-Lazare.

When he moved to Paris about 1922, 1923, his angle of vision
for his novels—his itineraries, his, as it were, literary
geography—of course isn't comparable to that of his native Le
Havre, but he's dealing with areas that are geographically circumscribed: there *is* a frontier, a very important one—that's the
River Seine, in its exit from Paris, as it moves, turgidly, its filthy
waters, in the direction of the estuary, in the direction of Rouen,
and Le Havre. With one exception, I think, all his novels about the
Paris region are novels about the banlieue Saint-Lazare, Rueil-
Malmaison, Bougival, Suresnes, all those semi-villages, semi-
suburbs that are approached on the electric line from the Gare
Saint-Lazare. Most of his novels, the ones that I most appreciate,

that's to say *Loin de Rueil* and *Pierrot mon ami*, are circumscribed in very limited and therefore very predictable areas. They are novels of reassurance, reassurance *à la petite échelle*—the scale is that of those maps you see outside French suburban stations, generally fixed onto a cement stand, *le planisphère de Rueil-Malmaison*, and so on. There's the Cimetière, Lycée, École Communale, Établissement *un tel*, distilleries or whatever; some small local industry, bottle factory or something, the small grid of streets, and the slaughterhouse, perhaps the *baignade*; because it will be on the river, there would be a *piscine*, using the river, and so on. And this, the very modest world geography of the ideal, or to me the ideal, Queneau novel, which is a novel of habit, habit seen through the day, as it were from dawn to dusk, with its fixed and almost invariable *points de chute*—*l'apéro*, *l'heure de l'apéritif*, followed by lunch *dans un petit restaurant*, followed by a visit to the *P.M.U.*, the Pari-Mutuel Urbain, because most of Queneau's rather modest heroes are what Queneau himself describes as *hippophile*, people very much given to betting on the French Tote, and they would never let a day pass without going to P.M.U.-Tabac and putting something on the *quatre heures et demie à Vincennes* or Longchamps or whatever, and so on through the day to the return generally to a lonely hotel room in a very quiet hotel, with names like l'Hôtel de l'Aveyron or l'Hôtel du Lot, in some quiet backstreet, a semi-rural, semi-suburban, semi-Parisian, individualistic, easy-to-circumscribe world of the '20s and '30s, and perhaps '40s—well before tower blocks, la Défense, and all this alien nightmarish geography which of course has very largely stifled the Queneau world, or the Dabit world—so that it is a period in time, very much; and I suppose for somebody of my generation, just as much as for Simenon, there is a *nostalgie des années trente*. This is where I come back to *les transports en communs* because the Queneau characters are not people that have their own transport, they're *les économiquement faibles*, and so that's where the Métro comes in; the Métro fascinates Queneau in a way that it has fascinated people like Aragon and some of the Surrealists. The sheer extraordinary juxtaposition of names, Sèvres-Babylone, Les Filles de Calvaire, Barbès-Rochechouart which has got such an extraordinary sort of *chuintement* about it, particularly when pronounced by a Parisian—this familiar and yet slightly poetical succession of stations, Queneau uses this very much in his poems; he's got a whole series of poems *on* the Métro, he's got some on *lignes d'autobus*, and he's got a whole series of poems on some of the more bizarrely named streets of Paris—things like l'impasse Jésus or la rue Dieu—so that there *is* movement and there's movement outside your *planisphère*, as it were, but you always come back and the movement is predictable, all part of the Queneau fantasy of the underground world of the Métro. When he has in these novels, these condensed biographies, a sort of Rake's Progress in four movements, as it were, and five tableaux, with the Paris accent—you know, *les tout petits emplois . . . et puis, la fin, loge de concierge* (that's the final employment), *plusieurs faillites, mariage avec une peau, divorce*, various *escroqueries—première escroquerie, seconde escroquerie, prison, la rédemption*, and so on . . . he uses, he draws for these things very largely on the sort of advertisements one would see in the Métro still in the '40s and '50s, for private detective agencies, generally for divorce cases, he's *always* getting them in—*enquêtes privées*—this is all part of the same Métro culture, along with the medical advertisements, those old-fashioned medical advertisements that you got so much in the '30s, *les pastilles de l'Abbé Fleury*—the idea that if some patent medicine has been invented by a priest, well, it's a sort of supreme guarantee and you will have a very old-fashioned-looking priest, generally with a mass of ecclesiastical white hair and an old-fashioned *jabot* with the red edge to it—all this is part of the Queneau world.

I think what Queneau has and Simenon hasn't, is this ability to render the spoken word on paper, get it right, he gets it right, . . . it's utterly convincing for anybody really who has spent any time *in* Paris, and most of the time I spent in Paris I was a bachelor and therefore was dependent very largely on the *restaurant d'habitués* not just for my meals but actually for my social enjoyments, because one would go round the tables: '*bonjour*', '*bonsoir*', and so on, and people would talk from one table to the other. Queneau has, I think, *marvellous* flair for recapturing conversations —family, children, what are you going to do at the week-end, the weather, a few references perhaps to events, but basically apolitical conversations, sometimes extremely *savoureux* in its vulgarity, and yet at the same time very polite—it is *la sociabilité française*, which used so much to attract eighteenth-century travellers to Paris, they didn't find it so rumbustious as you would in an English coffee-house or something, there were limits, there was dignity; if you were talking about your teenage daughter you wouldn't let out too much, it would be kept *au niveau des convenances*. I think this is quite brilliant in Queneau, it creates a total picture without the necessity of so much descriptive décor as you get in Simenon.

In *Pierrot mon ami*, the centre, really, of the geography is the old, permanent pleasure-palace, Luna-Park, which I think was built sometime in the 1900s, and you had a Big Wheel and all the usual things—dodgem cars, the Tunnel of Love, fakirs galore, fortune-tellers, the whole noise and blare and gunpowdery smell and sweat of a permanent fair-ground. It was situated just beyond the Porte Maillot, the rather fashionable end of Paris, and I think the residents of the *XVIme* must have been enormously glad when it all went up in flames in one night. *Pierrot mon ami* ends up with the description of the burnt-out Luna-Park and all the cardboard figures, how the sort of grease, the paint runs off them, this is the Surrealist element, Queneau himself obviously surveying the ruins with intense satisfaction and interest—all the submarine monsters upside down with their tails burnt off. It's got the whole rigmarole of those extraordinary Anglo-French names like L'Alpinic Railway, L'Admirable's Galerie, Le Palais de la Rigolade, and the dotty extravaganza of the fair-ground, with the *bizarreries* of juxtapositions that you get in French. And this appeals to Queneau, and he finds these extraordinary verbs—*débagouler*, to spout, to sick up: '*Le bonisseur . . . fit donc fonctionner le piqueupe qui se mit à débagouler Travadja la moukère et le Boléro de Ravel*'—and he *invents* verbs to get the sound of a barker doing his sales talk, introducing, and inviting, 'Come in, come in!'

In a way it has very much cinema qualities, so it seems to me, which of course *were* used in the rather different context of *Zazie dans le Métro*, which I don't find so attractive. Zazie herself is rather *m'as-tu-vue*, she's a very perverse little girl in some ways, and she doesn't have quite the freshness of the other juvenile characters in Queneau novels. One feels perhaps that Queneau himself has become slightly jaded by the '50s, some of the juvenile innocence has gone. I'm very fond of *Zazie* and I think it's the quintessence of something else in Queneau and that's his extraordinary ability to render spoken speech in print. You get this in the earlier novels, the ones written in the '30s and '40s, but the full sort of flowering of this extraordinary experimentation with getting the spoken word down in print is in *Zazie*. That's really, I think, what *Zazie*'s about. In Queneau's humour there's no cruelty, it always, I think even in *Zazie*, retains a sort of mixture of impudence, of the really naughty child, the impudent child, preferably speaking in a

Paris accent. Irreverent, irrepressible, *very* vulgar, but not in an un-pleasant way,.vulgar in its observations as well; Queneau is terribly funny when he describes his young hero in *Pierrot* making a pass at one of the girls who works in the Tunnel of Love; and he's going to meet her that evening, so there he is in the morning washing himself very carefully, as Queneau says, '*dans tous les endroits qui peuvent puer n'est-ce pas?*' And then there's the description of the over-powering scent of Uniprix Houbigant, of the girl's scent—I really don't think I know *any* writer who can get across the impact of smell so well, in aid of humour, generally, as a deflating process, as a process of taking the solemnity out of a situation. I don't think he fits into the tradition of French humour where laughter is directed against somebody or at the expense of somebody; French humour is something very acid, very Voltairian, really biting like an acid in-to metal—or the long tradition of almost the humour of hate, of Léon Bloy, Rochefort, later on Céline—Céline can be *extremely* funny because he too's got this ear, but ultimately he's not funny because you're just absolutely flattened by these monstrous ram-bling *delirious* sentences just *pouring* out bile; my reaction to Céline, particularly on re-reading something like *Voyage au Nord*, is 'Shut up! Belt up! Can't you ever lay off, can't you ever enjoy yourself?'—No, he can't. Queneau's humour is very French, though, in another respect, it *is* the humour of irreverence. Now, in *this* respect, I think Queneau does belong to a much wider, more ancient tradition of French humour which goes back to Villon; there's a certain Rabelaisian quality as well in his humour. It's a refusal to take *les personnages importants* at their own value, it's very much a puller-down of the national images: Le Chevalier Bayard—I'd love to know what Zazie would have made out of Le Général De Gaulle. In *Zazie* she says, '*Napoléon . . . Napoléon mon cul! Il m'intéresse pas du tout, cet enflé, avec son chapeau à la con.*' *Cet enflé. Cet enflé*—that's marvellous! Now, that's what I like! *Cet enflé. . . .* it's *l'humour du banal. Bānāl*, I suppose, with long a's of *les petites gens*. It's a mixture of the reassuring, vulgar, predictable—and occasionally some extraordinary phrase which is totally unexpected and hits you under the chin and you say, this is terribly funny. I can think of a case in point, when, in a hotel which is both a hotel and a *hôtel de passe* (where people are liable to go for very short periods), a man comes and says to the *caissière*, '*Je veux voir Maria.*' And she says, '*Vous pouvez pas voir Maria, elle est occupée.*' '*Mais, il est* indispensable *que je voie Maria.*' '*Im-*

possible!' And he insists. And she says, '*Elle est sous-homme.*' And it's the sheer, the *vulgarity* of the phrase that just hits you, it's like a totally unexpected tennis-shot, it really does hit you. And this is Queneau as a listener. . . . Parisian conversation *is* extremely inventive, and it can be very crude, of course. But not shocking! There's something very sunny, and almost sort of *printanier*, about Queneau. It's got a gentleness, I think, of the sort of sky, the Île de France on an April day, between showers and clouds and so on. It *can* be tempered with disaster, but it's not in any way a humour of catastrophe. Catastrophe is outside, because it's day-to-day stuff.

PART THREE

8

Ixelles

So far, I have been concerned with the works of French novelists and of novelists writing in French about particular localities at certain periods of time; and I have taken the specific case of Raymond Queneau as a novelist of habit, of fixed and restricted itineraries, and, thus, of reassurance, the reassurance to be derived from the sheer unpretentiousness and prudent timidity of *la vie à petite échelle* (in Queneau's case, that imposed by the Promenade, the *planisphère*, and the *ligne de métro*). If, to take another example, René Fallet and his young friends occasionally venture out of Villeneuve-Saint-Georges, on their Vespas, acquired in the full flush of post-Liberation optimism, to display themselves in Paris, their point of entry is predictably the pont de Charenton, their maximum penetration will be Strasbourg-Saint-Denis. Queneau's habitués can take a Sunday walk to the Bois de Sainte-Cucufa, just as an inhabitant of Viroflay will find himself impelled, as on the lines of a tramcar, upwards, to conclude at the ponds of Ville-d'Avray. Or a *petit-employé*, living in a large block of flats facing on the Ligne de Sceaux at Les Baconnets, will be drawn, Sunday afternoon, towards the concrete-bottomed ponds, the minuscule concrete-edged artificial islands, connected to the mainland by tiny exotic bridges in cement, disguised as rustic and gnarled wood, and decorated by doll's-house *châteaux-forts* also in cement, and painted red, yellow, blue and chocolate, to the Bois de Verrière. Likewise, *les Ibis*, a concrete-and-stucco-tamed jungle, the wild life provided by stone cranes and herons, bending forward in drinking position, three ponds, two islands, a footbridge in Japanese style, will draw out the family units from the neighbouring villas of Le Vésinet and Chatou. What itinerary could be more predictable, more reassuring, and more banal, than that of the *promenade de dimanche* in the suburbs of Paris!

I am reminded, too, of the monumental diary kept by a French archivist, in several scores of schoolboy notebooks (all marked

Préfecture de l'Oise), relating the clockwork mechanism of his inverted day: *me suis levé 18 h., me suis lavé 18h2, me suis habillé
18h5, ai mangé 2 tartines de pain d'épice 18h7, suis sorti sur le
Cours 18h12, ai suivi le chemin des remparts, ai croisé au niveau
du tabac M. un Tel, notaire, au gilet duquel il manquait le
troisième bouton en partant du bas 18h19, ne l'ai pas salué 18h20*,
and so on, day after day. In this instance, only the framework
remained, left behind to his successor, with empty tins of Abeille,
used for cooking, and rotting socks.

So I too want to propose the framework of a novel that has not
been written and that I will not be likely to write.

The framework is the commune of Ixelles, one of the nineteen independent municipalities which, together, form what is called *le
Grand Bruxelles*, or Greater Brussels. The period is from about
September 1944, after the liberation of the Belgian capital, until
sometime in the middle 1950s.

The axis of Ixelles, the chaussée d'Ixelles, runs steeply down
towards the Place Émile Flagey and then down towards two ponds.
The ponds, known to the local inhabitants as *les étangs d'Ixelles*,
are part of Brussels's lost river. They are edged with concrete and a
narrow sward enclosed by chains—the permissible terrain of ducks,
but not of couples or of children. The concrete paths round the
ponds offer two itineraries: the northern route, skirting the R.T.B.
building, the Maison de la radio, and the Église Sainte-Croix; and
the southern route, via the avenue du Général de Gaulle. Before
1945, this was called the avenue de la Cascade: the waterfall runs
through a concrete conduit from the upper pond into the lower
one, at the level of the causeway which divides the two ponds.

At the opening of these two routes, at the western tip of the
lower pond, is a very ornate statue, one I would describe as being in
le style Léopold II, together with a fountain that no longer works,
but which, at one time, must have been supplied with water from
the lower pond. The statue is of Till Eulenspiegel and was erected
in memory of Charles de Coster, the nineteenth-century Belgian
writer who made Till Eulenspiegel an incarnation of the Flemish
folk spirit. This statue is, I suppose, as reassuring to generations of
young Ixellois and Ixelloises as that of Peter Pan in Kensington Gardens is to young inhabitants of London.

Whichever route one takes, the paths lead implacably towards
the squat, chrome-coloured building of the Abbaye de la Cambre.
This is set in small, formal, seventeenth-century gardens, with box

hedges, an *orangerie* that is not doing very well in the damp climate, and three avenues of clipped trees. The central avenue was presumably for the local important people—*le gratin bruxellois* —and the two outer ones for the less important ones, *le menu peuple*.

It is possible to push on beyond the Abbaye de la Cambre: to climb the steep approach to the avenue Louise and thence to the Bois de la Cambre. Or it is possible to take an alternative route to the avenue Louise, a little lower down the street, reaching that particular *voie triomphale* of the Brussels upper bourgeoisie, at the level of La Taverne Louise, a very, very quiet place with plants in highly polished brass containers, and small alcoves in which there are tables bearing pink lampshades that give a pink tint to the pages of *Le Soir* and *La Dernière Heure*.

But the Abbaye de la Cambre is a frontier, an ultimate temple of reassurance at which most inhabitants of Ixelles will turn back homewards. They can, though, extend their limits, in the other direction, by going back up the chaussée d'Ixelles, to the Porte de Namur. This can be described as the checkpoint from the centre of Brussels into Ixelles, but I think the *maison communale*, the town hall, is a much better starting-point. This unpretentious, cream-coloured, three-storeyed building is clearly the centre of what is an identifiable small town, with its own *bourgmestre*, or burgomaster, and its own flag.

Les étangs d'Ixelles provide for the Ixellois a terrain designed for promenading, entertainment, deep conversation, vigorous exercise, meditation, and reading. Its iron or concrete seats provide opportunities for the closed conversation, *à deux*, of the approaches to love—the preliminary exploration of another person's life. The pram-borne population, too, has been given an ideal terrain. And, because of the presence of the very large and modern Église Sainte-Croix, it is a terrain for imposing funeral processions, headed by uniformed brass bands, playing Handel's Dead March from *Saul*, or the oddly unsuitable, fast-moving, and joyful 'La Brabançonne', the Belgian national anthem. Also to be seen are the early-morning and evening *pénitentes* and, on Sundays, families in groups, *en grappes*.

The complete itinerary, from the *maison communale* to the low-lying Abbaye de la Cambre, passes, as I have said, through the cascading chaussée d'Ixelles, which is a street lined with artisan establishments and small shops: *merceries, pâtisseries, ressemelage, blanchisserie, cordonnerie, papeterie, marchand de journaux*; shops selling the profusion of chocolate, tobaccos, cheroots, and small cigars that give to Brussels its specific rich odour and colour, and a great many cafés and *tavernes*: Stella Artois, Gueuse-Lambic, Bières de la Meuse. Interspersed between *le petit commerce* are the daily whitened front steps of dwelling-houses, more numerous in the village-like streets leading off the chaussée, rue du Couloir and others, small irregular houses in dark reds, whitewashed, cream-coloured to match the trams, lime-green, the windows picked out in black or in white surrounds, very solid, and low on the ground, with low roofs in curling red tiles; at the side of each door, two or three bells, with visiting cards beside each, bearing the double-names of families. It would be hard to find a more enclosed and predictable landscape: each artisan, each shopkeeper with a name, each householder with a double-name, each café and *taverne* containing its immutable clientèle, seen through the large windows at all hours, the numbers expanding with evening. At the upper end, between the Porte de Namur and the Place Communale, hangs a pervading and rather appetising smell of *frites*, the other component that, along with tobacco and chocolate, forms the specific and inimitable *parfum de Bruxelles*. The architecture of the chaussée itself, and even more of the streets at right angles to it, is semi-rural, such as might be encountered in the Tournésis, or in small towns like Leuze, on the road between France and the capital, or in villages in the Province de Namur, houses the plastic qualities and the even colour-washes of which—beige, russet, lime-green, cream, white, dark green and black, red and black—seem to cry out for an appropriate painter.

At the level of the ponds, the *étangs*, though, the árchitecture changes. It is either *style Léopold II*, the Belgian equivalent to High Victorian, or the ironwork fantasies of Brussels domestic architecture of the 1920s, which is a period that marked the city more permanently than any other capital—at least that I know. There is a kaleidoscope of stained glass in diamonds and lozenges, *modern-style* fretwork, and hints of a discreet, fussy, and, perhaps, rather uninspired Anglomania of a purely bourgeois variety.

If the chaussée d'Ixelles is *artisanale*, the area adjacent to the *étangs d'Ixelles* is solidly professional middle-class, while the Abbaye de la Cambre keeps to itself, at the far end, surviving as a reminder of Flemish Gothic, with rather heavy but simple seventeenth- and eighteenth-century additions.

The chaussée d'Ixelles is the street that supplies all the basic family needs of the Ixellois; it is the equivalent to the main street of a provincial town. Though its walls are often covered with election posters, it would be very hard to discover an urban landscape more obviously unrevolutionary. Instead, there is the enclosed, protected, gradually discoverable domain of habit, prudent friendship, careful observation of the kind that addresses itself to the whiteness of the front step or to the brilliance of a brass door-knocker. Violence is controlled, with a recognised vocabulary of mounting insult, and is confined to the later hours of a Saturday night. The results are little more than broken glasses, broken chairs, and an exchange of blows.

To emphasise both the provinciality, the continuity, and the sturdy individualism of the family unit, Ixelles contains an unusually high proportion of domestic pets: dogs that, on Saturdays, get drunk with their masters; cats in attitudes of comfortable and possessive repose on front steps and window-sills; canaries and other tiny bright-coloured birds are displayed in elaborate cages in windows emphasised by a fringe of lace curtain. Unrevolutionary, self-confident, slightly old-fashioned and dowdy, Ixelles has been quite untouched by the ugly mushrooming of the nearby *quartier de l'Europe*, the area of the offices of the European Community.

The itinerary of Ixelles is one to be explored at dawn, when the mist is still lying over the ponds of the Abbaye de la Cambre, before even the dustcarts are out, and only those who have worked through the night are enjoying the peculiar luxury of a walk through the sleeping commune. A few yellow lights of cafés are already showing, a couple of ghostly trams huddle together and wait in the Place Émile Flagey, and a scattering of lights can be seen at the top of the otherwise black and gloomy Maison de la Radio. A night-worker on the treadmill of the Saint-Nicolas trade or of that of Easter, has ready for delivery to L'Innovation, the chain store in the rue Neuve, a score of freshly painted toys. He is his own master and, like an eighteenth-century artisan, able to regulate his life to his own lonely, eccentric pattern of work, deadened even to the hourly changing sounds of the working day.

This is the hour at which, all at once, birds break into twittering and song, the ducks take their heads from under their wings and fly into the waters of the ponds, and the seabirds appear from the north, a reminder of how close the area is to a sandy, indented coast, and to the wandering inlets of the anarchical river Schelde.

The hour approaching daybreak is the moment when cities show themselves in a different way from that seen in broad daylight. In Ixelles, privileged walkers see, deployed for their exclusive enjoyment, the squat contours cut out in the silhouette of the Abbaye de la Cambre; the modern Église Sainte-Croix with a disguise of the unpretentious outlines of a purely rural church; and the radio building lends the brooding menace of a place of torture, a place where terrible things happen in the night, the evidence of which is removed in the morning, along with the empty cigarette-packets and ash.

The pre-dawn light also reveals the stately magnificence of an empty and silent avenue Louise, stretching out to a full length, like an exercise in perspective, and its solid houses still dark cliffs, enclosing a black macadam stream.

These are the timid openings of a new day; one, for most, so full of hope, but also one displaying, like the offerings left, blandly and as if in laughter, on an early-morning beach by the receding tide, the unbearable evidence of crimes committed under cover of night. At the approach to the avenue Louise, a tiny hand protrudes from the lid of a crammed dustbin, in front of an affluent, unsympathetic, tall, and over-ornate apartment block. When the lid is removed, a minute, doll-like, quite naked girl is revealed—a diminutive Bruxelloise-to-be that never saw the day.

And so there still lingers fear in an itinerary so reassuring in full daylight, when the gardens of the *abbaye*, in the hesitant half-light still dark jungles, are swept clear of mystery and of the suspected presence of objects hideous to see.

Apart, then, from the night-worker and his companions—those who sat up with him, as he worked at his lathe—who will see the urban dawn? First of all, the dying who, somehow, have managed to live through the night, not by choice, but from the doubtful mercy of relentless biological processes; secondly, the parents, husbands, wives, children, close friends of the recently dead who have been awakened at this hour by the incessant ringing of the telephone, followed by the implacable, unanswerable short sentence. The mourner dresses hurriedly and rushes out into the silent streets in search of a taxi, to reach one of the vast hospitals on the periphery of the city—a building which is a mass of lights and enveloping warmth, a building which never sleeps.

Murder and death have taken place before the city has done its toilet and has tidied away such inadmissible and disturbing secrets.

The dawn itinerary offers the reassurance of an entirely predictable movement, hour by hour, as Ixelles, like a lightly sleeping
Gulliver, slowly stirs from slumber. It stretches an arm or leg, sending out, like a prudent advance guard, a brightly lit single tram, its
destination board shining a filmy yellow and black in the half-light,
or sending out a fast-moving postal van, with a golden hunting-
horn on its side.

Another advance guard is a boy on an elaborate bicycle. It has
many gears, with a *dérailleur*, and has handlebars shaped like
curling ram's horns. A kingfisher flash of yellows, blues, and
greens, the boy threads his machine through the still lighted streets,
delivering here *Le Drapeau Rouge*, there *La Libre Belgique*. Each
will have its readers in neighbouring houses in the same street.

In 1944 and 1945, the windows of those houses sprouted un-
accustomed adornment, a rival to green plants in brass pots or to
brightly coloured birds in cages: photographs of Léopold III in a
general's uniform, or of his brother, Prince Charles, *en civil*, in
mufti, announced, like flags, contrary allegiances. It says much for
the placidity of the Ixellois that none of these windows was ever
broken. In any case, there would not have been any point, as
everybody knew, even without such display, where his neighbours
stood on *la question du roi*: *Léopoldiste* or *anti-Léopoldiste*.

The huge tricolour flag flies reassuringly limp in the morning
cold, or cracks merrily in the east wind, over the *palais du roi*.
Delicious smells of rich coffee and of chocolate emerge from the
early *crémeries* of the chaussée d'Ixelles. One or two *pâtissiers*, still
in the white overalls and white caps of nightwork, can be seen
coming out into the street to put the handles on the outside doors of
their shops.

The ornamental gates of the Bois de la Cambre, surmounted by
two lazy, yawning lions, are already open. The lions, each on top
of his plinth, lie spread out, with claws outstretched, inviting
isolated groups of men and women exercising their dogs, and
athletes and enthusiasts running downhill through the mist,
towards the big lake, which is still a great, whitish hole, like an
inverted cloud, and soon lost to the sight of the runners as they
disappear down the straight avenue of ghostly trees.

Perhaps if it is the specifically silent dawn of a Sunday, with
an extra quality of stillness, accentuated by the absence of bustle,
there might also be seen stepping gingerly along the chaussée
d'Ixelles, holding on to walls, projections, and cornices, zigzagging

uncertainly, as if deprived of rudder and internal gyroscope, a few rather battered figures, men in caps or dented bowlers, their feet catching in their woollen scarves. The debris of a Saturday night spent in the rue Haute or in other warm and noisy pleasure-spots of the Quartier des Marolles, they are now washed towards home. Now they are in search of an ultimate drink, to enable them to put on a better countenance to a questioning or shruggingly resigned household. Or lonely British soldiers, cleared right out down below by implacably systematic Luxembourgeoises—contents of pockets, cigarettes, pay book, for Brussels is one of the world capitals of *faux papiers*, and any *pièce d'identité* will have an immediately negotiable value, there and then, *derrière le comptoir* or, at the most remote, at a café round the corner—and so full of anger and belgophobia, people best avoided, as they grope their way, shouting incoherent threats in thick Glaswegian, to the Leave Centres that, at one time, in post-Liberation years, existed Place Sainte-Croix, a population unwelcome and fortunately transient, the presence of which, in my own account, is merely designed to fix a given locality in a specific point of time. Soldiers—save the rare Red Army ones—appeared incongruous among the solidly and tranquilly civilian population of the *commune*, a place that, one felt, would have liked, like so many of its unambitious inhabitants, to have lived right outside great events, or, at worst, on their more distant fringes.

But when I go back to Brussels and to Ixelles now, I find my narrative has been interrupted. There has been a death, perhaps several deaths, creating, here and there, holes behind façades, putting new, unfamiliar names on shop signs, new figures behind elaborately polished counters, serving new drinks, and making of myself a stranger all the more lost and wistful, once back in the geography so utterly familiar and apparently untouched.

A family, having lost the carpenter head of the household, has had a series of moves. At first, it was a series of moves within Ixelles, away from the comfortable familiarity of the rue du Couloir, in which the only previous move had been from one side of the street, No 19, to the house immediately opposite, No 24, a change entailing the rise from basement to ground-floor level. The next move, however, had been to an address one or two streets nearer to the Place Sainte-Croix, and to the ponds.

This family of toymakers had always managed so well to live outside conventional time, outside work discipline, out of reach of the media, indeed, well beyond most collectivities, huddled within an underground of semi-basement or contiguous *rez-de-chaussée*, or on-the-level-with-the-street, topography. It was unthinkable, for instance, to imagine them living on even the first floor or having friends who reached up to such heights. It was as if a staircase leading upwards beyond the ground floor had always been something quite beyond their common experience.

They enjoyed a very exclusive circle of friendship, based on a rare combination of individualism and eccentricity, though eccentricity quite unstudied because it was quite unconscious, because they simply did not judge people as other people might have judged them, being totally, indeed quite joyfully, immune to the power of emulation and to the pull of envy. They were people joined together by relative lack of success, who could only move downhill, as if drawn to the ponds and to the church by the force of gravity.

Perhaps, too, the move farther downhill had been due to a veritable *dégringolade*, a tumble, as a result of the loss of the leading carpenter, the small master of the fragile yet utterly contented enterprise of toymaking for L'Innovation, the chain store in the rue Neuve. Or perhaps it had been dictated in some way by the *curé* of Sainte-Croix, about the only person vaguely in a position of authority from whom these people were willing to take advice and from whom, every now and then, out of the toy season, when there was little demand for toys, they would accept help beyond such meagre benefits as they may have drawn from the Belgian state.

Then, all at once, or so I gathered as I called here and there, ringing bells against which there were still familiar names, they had moved away completely, right out of Ixelles into an almost alien Uccle, and a long way beyond the frontier of the avenue Louise. The reasons I do not know, save that they must have been awful, and compelling.

Perhaps the move was dictated by need, perhaps also by some steady, implacable change in the social composition of Ixelles, no doubt subjected to pressures from below the hill, from the invasive, pitiless marshlands of *l'Europe*, sending predatory outriders of Eurocrats up the heights and then down the chaussée d'Ixelles, driving out the artisans and shopkeepers and independent folk and giving over the doll's-house-like buildings to readers of fashionable left-wing weeklies and fortnightlies.

I could, however, vaguely recall that Uccle had not been totally alien territory, at least to the carpenter's wife. She had been in the habit of going there once a month, to see the *commanditaire*, the sleeping partner, of the toymaking enterprise, a middle-class lady who was occasionally referred to, in deferential but quite impersonal terms, and who, for reasons that remained obscure, had something to do with the ebb and flow—more ebb than flow nine months of the year—of orders for the home-made wooden toys. Perhaps then, in the last resort, it had been this mysterious figure who had come to the rescue and had been the cause of the move to Uccle.

The façades of Ixelles are still much the same, but I no longer know what lies behind them. I can no longer look down through the iron grating of an area, to spy friends in a lighted room below ground. I can only walk alone in streets that were once inhabited by people I knew.

So I have, indeed, the *cadre*, the elementary framework, of a novel—one well set in time and place: the second half of the 1940s and the early 1950s, in the Commune of Ixelles. But how to conclude it? It simply peters out in emptiness, absence, indifference, and uncertainty: '*Oh . . . ils sont partis; il y a longtemps de cela. On ne sait pas où.*' Or: '*Cela ne doît pas être bien loin. C'était après que le fils a fait son service.*'

Left behind, and pathetically intact, is much of the décor; also, perhaps, a few scattered witnesses to the warmth, simplicity, and generosity of lives one once tentatively shared and explored. But life, change, ageing, readjustment to the sense of loss, do not respond to such artistic imperatives as might be dictated by personal memory and by the desire to take up the book again, perhaps after years of neglect, at the page at which one had left off.

The Commune d'Ixelles which I have tried to immobilise, at a precise point in time, I could then have peopled with a very enriching and completely illogical collectivity of *marginaux*, of marginal people, marginal because their ties did not, in any way, respond to the orthodoxies of sociology, or politics, or common origins, or trade, or professional relations, or even sports activities, or shared leisure (only the father and the son took to the *pistes cyclables*, for trips to Malines and Antwerp, an enthusiasm not shared either by the wife or by their generally sedentary friends, one of the most regular of whom no sooner mounted a bicycle than he fell off it); all they really had in common was a commendable ability to exist quite outside any known or accepted orthodoxy.

It is a story that has moved on without consulting me, but still leaving me with a heritage of enrichment, and with the warmth of once shared experience—a great deal of it bizarre, most of it quite outside the ordinary run of things.

Perhaps this is all one can ask of a place: to be the reassuring *cadre* of past exploration, and of the memory of common friendship and shared reactions over a regular, predictable, but inverted pattern of night and day—the febrile industry of November and December, and again of March and April; the terrible doldrums of a long, long summer and early autumn, with meals of bread, butter, *saucisson*, and coffee—beerless months.

We all live with history, and we live in history, and the frontiers between history and imagination are very little more than Chinese screens, removable at will. And a historian is a person who walks his chosen itineraries with his eyes open. It is up to the novelist to pick up the pieces, to tie up the loose ends, and to cap the edifice with a conclusion suited to what has gone before.

I have lingered in Ixelles, as much as anything else, in search of myself and my friends and of their compact circle. I have lingered in search of those who, during the German occupation, opted for the wrong side, without full awareness of what they were doing. It might have been merely for a pair of long leather boots, a very rare and prestigious luxury in the Belgium of 1942, or to satisfy some minor, passing, personal craving—for chocolate, tobacco, or coffee. It might have been motivated by the desire to get even with some Jewish middleman for an imagined economic ill dating back to the late 1930s. All these actions were forgivable because the people who did them were basically innocent; indeed, eventually, these people were forgiven. I have lingered as much in search of them as of, as yet, an unwritten *roman ixellois* or, in the wider but surely more profitable context of the very largely inexistent *roman belge*.

Neither, of course, is for me, a historian, a witness, and a fellow-traveller with those whose greatest ambition was to be left alone to go their own, mainly unsuccessful way, to write. All I can do is to sketch in the framework, and to set up the stage sets and the scenery.

I can provide perhaps a dozen or so characters: Jean and Émilie; Poum, their son; Marcel; Charles; *la femme de Charles* (she did not appear to have had any other name); Reinette, Marcel's girl-friend; Marcel's mother (an extremely long-suffering woman); *le Cosaque*, a constant inhabitant of a fantasy world far removed from the rue du Couloir.

I can add a suggested chronology that is bizarre because it is mostly back-to-front, turning night into day, with the passage of the night-hours witnessed from below street level. I can even provide a basic dialogue of *'belgicismes'*, illustrating a naïve and insistent nationalism, neither Walloon nor Flemish, nor even *bruxellois*, not even purely *ixellois*, but specifically Belgian; a nationalism one associates with small and rather self-conscious countries.

Then I can complete it with a topography that will include a childhood in Namur, a mother unidentified, but supposedly from the German-speaking enclave round Eupen (Jean's mother); another purely rural childhood in Marienbourg, of farming stock, and looking it (Émilie); common origin in Charleroi, with matching accent (Marcel and Reinette); Ixelles-born Charles and *la femme de Charles*; in the case of Jean, an apparently unrelated succession of jobs, including various unspecified ones in the port quarter of Antwerp, despite a total lack of Flemish.

There would be the seasonal descent to L'Innovation, and occasional sorties down to the Quartier des Marolles, in search of collective enjoyment. Long walks would be taken, right through the Bois de la Cambre, to the *commune* of Boitsfort or even to the forest of Groenendael.

Finally, there would be the fabulous and never-to-be-forgotten adventure of *l'Exode*, in the summer of 1940, ending with six months or more in a sunny vineyard and small farm somewhere in the Département du Gers, in the south-west of France. This is an event which, through the years, has acquired the expanding proportions of a legend, endlessly repeated and embellished, and involving the earliest experience of the then infant Poum. A desire is often expressed to return to the Gers, to thank the farmer and his family, but this desire will never be realised because it is quite unrealisable.

Back, then, to reality, to the rue du Couloir and the firmly marked frontiers of that small enclave, the Commune d'Ixelles, a coloured island in a multi-coloured agglomeration of nearly a score of other municipal republics, forming that strange, shapeless, and disputatious entity, gradually eating up the surrounding Flemish countryside, of *le Grand Bruxelles*.

And there is that even stranger, more varied federation of city states joined together by rich farmlands and by many watercourses, sandy pine forests, abandoned *corons*, or mining villages, like cities of the desert, pyramidal coal wastes, strung together by trams, buses, and trains of the C.F.B., the last two marked merely 'B', the most convincing of national affirmations.

The *royaume de Belgique* itself is a quilted patchwork of immense historical variety, tied together as much by intermarriage across the linguistic borders, by common cultural attitudes, by common reactions to others, and, above all, by common reactions to immediate neighbours: the Dutch are an object of constant criticism—a mean lot, given to endless litigation on the subject of the navigation of the Schelde; the French are seen as arrogant, patronising, and even sneering; and there is a common indifference to most other nationalities.

This reaction to others is characterised, too, by a certain *esprit frondeur*; a desire never to be taken in; a very basic common sense; a refusal to be unduly impressed, whether by uniform, titles, or literary reputations; a large reserve of scepticism; a sense of humour, inclined to the scatological; drinking habits that tend to be uninhibited and, above all, very noisy; an appetite always considerable and normally not easily satisfied; a monarchy which is touchingly popular and middle-class.

Perhaps Ixelles is, at this very moment, secreting its own novelist. Or perhaps all such potential witnesses have become self-elected *émigrés*, who have moved west, right out of the comforting, and backbiting, circle of restricted national experience and national bickering, to evoke Ixelles with deprecatory laughter, and with apologies for a garment unfashionably provincial, despite its modern cut, and so to be discarded in the artificial, rather wearisome conformity of a zealously adopted Parisian ambiance, speech, attitude, and condescension.

9
Marseilles

The place of Marseilles in French literature is rather an ambivalent and a contrasting one, in that it figures in very different aspects. On the one hand, it is, first of all, a *lieu de passage*, a place to pass through, coming or going; and, on the other hand, it is a somewhat secretive resident community—a place to live in.

In the 1930s and, I think, until quite recently, Marseilles has been good for a laugh, at least with Parisians; indeed, one might even say this was part of the city's export industry, along with soap and cooking oil, via Marcel Pagnol and his creations—Marius, Fanny, and César—and, of course, those two great actors and comedians, Fernandel and Raimu. And, again, there are the joke picture postcards of conversations on the Canebière, which is the main street of Marseilles, leading down to the port, at the Quai des Belges.

I am sometimes tempted to think that the joke was actually on the Parisians: the inhabitants of Marseilles especially thriving under this convenient disguise of levity, loquacity, and mendacity, 'talking big', exaggerating, telling what the locals call *la galéjade*—the tall story. *La galéjade*, seen as a national southern characteristic, must have satisfied in some way the very relative verbal sobriety and reticence of the native-born Parisian, and of those recently converted to 'Parisianism'.

The mixture of much-publicised corruption and inefficiency, however, that seemed to characterise the municipality, the police, the *Renseignements généraux*, the fire brigade,[1] and the Prefecture of the Bouches-du-Rhône, as revealed in such national events as the burning down of the Hôtel de Noailles, boulevard d'Athènes, or the assassination, on the Canebière, of King Alexander of Jugoslavia and Louis Barthou, undoubtedly served to harden this Parisian vision of *manque de sérieux* when applied to the Second City (and

---

[1] Though doubts about its efficiency could be expressed also by inhabitants. ' "Tant que nous aurons une mairie socialiste," ' states Pagnol's uncle, Jules, ' "il n'y aura pas de pompiers. Je l'ai dit cent fois à Joseph." Et c'était vrai, car il l'avait dit un jour sur la terrasse, en lisant son journal . . . (Marcel Pagnol, *Le Temps des secrets*).'

there was even some suggestion of fraud arising out of that claim). It was also a comfortable way of discrediting, at least to one's own satisfaction, a place that, throughout its immensely rich history, had shown itself again and again quite capable of living and prospering in the *absence* of Paris and *without* Paris. Certainly, as a result of such firmly held attitudes, there was little hope of any eminent Marseillais (at least since Thiers) ever being taken seriously in the capital, as some of the leading Protestant politicians from the port were later to discover to their disadvantage. Indeed, twenty years or so after the king's murder, the appointment, as an *expert*, in one of Marie Besnard's three trials, of a Marseillais toxicologist, with the unfortunate name of Médaille, was taken, by pretty well the whole of the Parisian press, as a guarantee that the *enquête* would go wrong, as, indeed, it did.[1] I can recall, too, at the time of the Liberation, the genuine indignation of my friends in Roubaix, people of widely different political beliefs, at the appointment, as Commissaire Régional du Nord, of a Marseillais; the Nord, they would complain bitterly, was a serious place, where people *worked*.

Indeed, I think what may further have contributed to this Parisian—and more generally northern—myth about the Second City and its inhabitants, extending it downwards to include Belleville, Ménilmontant, Clichy, and the industrial suburbs, was the creation of the *congés payés* in the summer of 1936. *La cité phocéenne*—already established as a particularly hoary joke, the North French equivalent of a shaggy-dog story—now further became associated, especially in retrospect, with leisure, with holidays, with walking about and taking the air, with eating squids in the sun or swimming off one of the little, rather dusty beaches, below the Pharo. The Parisian holiday-maker, whether clerk or metalworker, in typical Parisian imperialism, could only assume that, as *he* was on holiday, everyone else must be similarly occupied, indeed, that the whole of Marseilles, in its vast bowl facing seawards, had been especially laid out as a pleasure-ground for his benefit. And it would have been most unlikely that he would ever have torn himself away from the *corniches*, the Vieux Port, and the quai des Belges, to climb up to visit a soap factory in Saint-Louis.

In the late '30s, according to accepted Parisian lore, particularly as then expressed in *Le Canard Enchaîné*, a paper designed to

[1] See my book *A Second Identity* (1969), 'The Memoirs of Marie Besnard', pp. 287-95.

acclimatise the provincial *instituteur* or *professeur de lycée* new to the city to the prejudices of *le bon ton parisien*, certain towns and the inhabitants of certain provinces had as their principal function to contribute to the formation of a sort of joke map of *l'Hexagone* (*Le Canard* would have more readily compared its shape to that of a schoolboy's *carte de France* on the sheet). The mere mention of the name Perpignan would release shock waves of hilarity: the very name, the accent, the alleged nature of the inhabitants, eternally *figés* as twentieth-century retarded Tartarins, wearing panamas or floppy berets, clothed from head to foot in colonial tussore, sipping *pastis*, playing pétanque, sitting arguing under the plane-trees, certainly never working or doing anything useful or serious, nor ever seen in the company of women, a purely masculine world, then, of boastful idleness and empty eloquence, barely living, and on what one could not tell. The sole function of the Perpignannais (not declinable in the feminine), it would seem, was to provide constant entertainment to the Paris-based schoolteacher, shopkeeper, *petit employé*, and intellectual. Much later in life, I was quite amazed to encounter in that town men with grave faces who never laughed and who dressed in black from head to foot, learned scholars and local historians, and teachers who devoted themselves to their work, about which they went with an air of austere gravity.

Perpignan was *the* joke town of the '30s (and perhaps it had already held that position in the previous decade). But there were plenty of others, most of them situated somewhere in the Midi, or in the Massif Central, and some in Brittany, particularly in the *bretonnant* part of it (*Le Canard*, angling above all for a teaching readership, was one of the most effective instruments of French linguistic imperialism), and some again in Alsace, providing the paper and its readers with the everlasting joy of taking off the German accent in French, the open vowels and the *ang* endings of the different Midis, the alleged *chuintement* of the Auvergnats, and Norman peasant renderings of -*oir*. *All* peasants were more or less comical, all wore clogs, country priests always wore long, protruding shovel hats, all country churches had Norman-type wooden spires, surmounted by huge weather-cocks that indicated north for south. And villages were awarded standard comic names. Some towns were funnier than others. Limoges was always good for a laugh, even declining and sprouting out into a small vocabulary: *limoger*, *limogeage*, a reference to Boulanger's posting in the previous century, and a relic, perhaps, of an even older horror of banishment dating back to the eighteenth century (and *what* punishment could be more dreadful than such removal from the centre of the universe?). So Romorantin would likewise qualify as an undesirable place of exile, a *voie de garage* to be avoided ('*je n'irai pas à Romorantin*'). Much the same could be said of the horrors of Gap, Mende, or Privas, Châteauroux, Langres, or Chaumont. *Aller à Niort* represented an ancient play on words, while Brussels was everlastingly associated with Mlle Beulemans, as well as with the midnight train from the Gare du Nord that would take the murderer, his hands still covered in blood, the swindler, and the burglar beyond the reach of French justice, adding the suggestion that one would never go to the Belgian capital for any reason other than to escape. Toulon also would provoke irresistible hilarity, at a period when its leading and extremely picturesque politician bore the extraordinary name of Escartefigue.

Equally indicative was the *absence* of certain towns and certain provinces from this apparently changeless map. There was nothing funny about Rouen, nor about Lille and the industrial towns of the north-east and the east. And if Dijon and Beaune would come in for a certain amount of good-natured ribaldry on the subject of wine-growing (*Le Canard*, a twentieth-century Père Duchesne, tended to equate libation with masculinity, promoting on its way the everlasting merits of *Juliénas*), Nevers and Moulins would not, perhaps because they would have appeared as too visibly melancholy. And there was Midi and Midi. The comic *méridional* belonged, by right, to the south-east rather than to the south-west; certainly Bordeaux and Toulouse were well out of the comic zone, whereas Nice, Toulon, the whole of Corsica (*Le Canard* was inexhaustible on the subject of the islanders), Orange, and Carpentras were in it. As far as the Auvergne was concerned, Parisian humour would be directed at the *bougnat* from a rural area; the Auvergnat was the peasant *par excellence*, and so there would be nothing particularly funny about the Michelin factory worker of Clermont-Ferrand. In the geography of Parisian attitudes and humour, the Midi did not extend even up to Valence. As for Lyons, the deep-seated suspicion in which Parisians had long held the city would not have allowed it any such light-hearted favour. There was, apparently, absolutely nothing funny about Lyons, nor about the Lyonnais.

But a mixture of Parisian arrogance and Parisian lack of curiosity is far from being alone to blame for the propagation of a largely mythical Marseilles, strictly *article d'exportation*, often consciously erected as a barrier to keep strangers out, and bearing about as much contact with reality as a Blackpool beach postcard has with the daily lives of the inhabitants of that other seaside town.

The result of this has been that the only truly evocative novelist of Marseilles, apart from Pagnol, was a Swiss, Blaise Cendrars, who first approached the port from the sea. He took a line on the Fort Saint-Jean, on the left-hand side of the harbour, and was guided in from far out in the Mediterranean by the tower of Notre-Dame-de-la-Garde with its immense statue of the Virgin, the rocky, brownish-red hills, covered in scarlet undergrowth, beyond, a reminder, at least to the historian, that the old bandit country, the nightly killing country of the White Terror, at the end of the eighteenth century,[1] extended right down to the fringes of the town, the market-gardens and orchards of the upper slopes of the bowl, right down to the level of the main road east to Aubagne, as if, landwards, Marseilles had been surrounded by a desert of another sort of alarm and hazard. Cendrars came in the same way as that recommended by the Abbé Expilly;[2] and he had the same intimate, almost loving knowledge of the prevailing winds blowing off the dangerous sea, or, on the contrary, tearing down the Rhône Valley,[3] making the approach nearly always dangerous, as the nautical-minded southern priest. For Cendrars, then, the port quarter was a temporary place of rest and relaxation and sunny enjoyment, an escape from loneliness, a plunge into verbal sociability, between long voyages, or from service in the Legion, or from various adventures in the valley of the Orinoco. If Marseilles belongs to *anyone*, apart from its own secretive inhabitants, it would be to the white-capped *légionnaires*, the honoured freemen of the old Vieux Port, and certainly recognised as such by the

[1] And, indeed, according to folk memory, much later. There must have been some background of reality to Pagnol's ghostly Grand Félix, who was said to have haunted the *pinèdes* above the city in the early years of the present century: '. . . il avait au moins mille moutons. Des bandits l'ont assassiné; ils lui ont planté un grand poignard entre les épaules et ils lui ont pris un gros sac de pièces d'or. Alors, il revient tout le temps, pour se plaindre, et il cherche son trésor . . . (*Le Château de ma mère*)'.

[2] L'abbé Jean-Joseph d'Expilly (1719-93), author of the celebrated *Dictionnaire géographique, historique et politique des Gaules et de la France*, Paris, 6 vols. 1762-1770. See under *Marseille*, *Martigues*, and *Provence*. The abbé is particularly informative on the subject of the prevailing winds off the sea or the shore and on the currents at the entrance to harbours.

[3] '. . . Toujours les petits pins au tronc noué penchés dans le sens du mistral, et les grandes dalles de pierres bleues.' (Marcel Pagnol, *La Gloire de mon père*.)

prostitutes of the rue Nationale, the rue des Couteliers, and the rue du Petit-Saint-Jean. This was where the Legion, even more than the *fusiliers-marins*, or the old colonial regiments, enjoyed *droit de cité*. Cendrars, a former member of the Foreign Legion and a tireless traveller, a man never for long on land, and then only on the very edge of land, was a particularly well-qualified observer of the small cafés and the tiny restaurants, their dark entrances protected by fringes of green matting, decorated with coloured beads, and of the varied inhabitants of the anarchical Vieux Port. His novels, which are really autobiographical novels, *L'Homme foudroyé*, *La Main coupée*, and his other tirelessly picaresque works, ranging from the Mediterranean to the Canal Zone, from northern Russia in the throes of revolution to Venezuela and the northern tip of the Latin-American continent, offer an always utterly convincing picture of place and people, of the influence of environment on a permanent or on a transient population; a picture as well observed, warm, and fraternal as the scenes set in Braïla, another great port near a vast delta, described, in novel after novel, with tenderness, compassion, and humour by Panaït Istrati, another traveller and regional novelist, who likewise wrote only in French—rather than in his native Rumanian (or Greek)—when attempting to describe a remarkably free childhood and adolescence spent in the harbour area, the markets, and the gypsy encampments of a port on the Black Sea.

The Swiss writer is completely at home in the steep little streets that lie in the shadow of the Hôtel de Ville and the cathedral. But his observation does not extend very far inland, not even as far as the fashionable shopping centre of the Quartier de la Bourse, the Préfecture, and the great shopping street, rue Saint-Ferréol, and so his work has become very much a period piece, an eloquent but sad monument to yet something else that has been lost: the sunny, salty, peppery, aromatic fraternity of a maritime community, well adjusted to the comings and goings of sailors, fishermen, colonial troops—a community facing seawards and resolutely turning its back on the hinterland.

With the decline of the importance of Marseilles as a great trading port, as the point of departure and arrival of colonial troops, administrators, and adventurers plying between France, Africa, and the Far East, with the shrivelling up of much of the Mediterranean inshore fisheries, most of the city of Cendrars and, indeed, of the city of the plays of Pagnol, has entirely disappeared.

Even the Greek fishermen seem to have left the Quai des Belges, to make way for tourists from the north and for extremely expensive fish restaurants and hotels and apartment blocks advertised '*avec vue sur le port*'.

One can hardly look forward to the further development of a maritime literature concerning giant petrol-carriers, as they ply between the oil fields of the Middle East and the Étang de Berre; and a present-day Conrad, a Loti, a Peisson, or a Cendrars would clearly be overtaken, and made completely irrelevant, by the constant speeding up of air transport (Marignane never occurs in any work either of Pagnol or of Cendrars), something that has killed the excitement of slow discovery, as made from offshore, or on foot inland, and that has reduced great waterfronts and once busy port areas to desolate industrial wastes of abandonment and rusty cranes. The Marseilles of the old *pont transbordeur*, as depicted, for instance, in an unforgettable sequence in *Un Carnet de Bal*,[1] seems now about as remote as the Paris of René Clair, the posters of Paul Colin (including that, representing the prow of a ship, for the Foire de Marseille), and that distant, almost fabulous period of French urban history when strange, rather frightening '*tomates*' performed, with a wonderfully realistic jerky mechanism, with a hideously contrived fixed and automatic smile, as if painted on, accompanied by a drilled rolling of the eyes, in the windows of shops: immaculate, in double-breasted suit, hat, and polished shoes, as they pointed, at carefully measured periodical intervals, to the designated object of wonder and envy, to the mixed delight and terror of small Parisian children, in coloured smocks and berets, their *cartables* strapped on their backs, in the '20s and '30s. The *tomates* were so appealing, and yet so alarming, because they really *did* seem to respond to a hidden machinery, and because no amount of juvenile provocation, whether by word or by telling gesture, would make them lose their fixed clownlike grin, their hideous smile, make them alter the steep arch of their permanently amazed eyebrows, or cause them to abandon the jerkily mechanical slow progress of their movements from front to side, the arm with the pointed hand being projected as it were by the vibrating movement of the whole body. And yet one knew, in one's heart of hearts, that they really *were* human, just poor men who had chosen this peculiar way of earning a sort of living, and who, when the lights went out and the blinds and shutters came down, would step

[1] Film directed by Julien Duvivier, 1937.

nimbly down from the shop-window, stretch themselves, scratch, resume the normal irregular flow of movement, before walking off to the nearest Bouillon Chartier, where, had it not been for their frayed and formal elegance, nothing would have distinguished them from the general mass of eaters who, in their speed to fill themselves with a poor fare, would themselves assume a mechanical movement of jaw and tongue itself reminiscent of the public performance just completed in the face of the street.

What, in French, one would call *la littérature de l'escale*—the literature of arrival and departure by sea—is thus as unlikely to experience a renewal in Marseilles as it would in Bordeaux or in Le Havre. Just as there is no longer any possibility of escape—and perhaps redemption—for Pépé-le-Moko,[1] or for some Parisian murderer, on the other side of the Pyrenees, in the cosmopolitan dockland of Barcelona or Algiers, the criminal on the run is unlikely to find a semi-clandestine berth on a tramp steamer bound out of Le Havre for the Canal Zone. MacOrlan, as much as Cendrars, has been overtaken by new forms of transport that have likewise destroyed the mysterious possibilities of the extinct Orient Express, the moving terrain of Paul Morand and Maurice Dékobra, of the *dame des sleepings* and the *contrôleur des wagons-lits* (a 1930-style Figaro), or the *salons dorés* of ocean-going liners. As an *invitation au départ*, Marseilles now has very little to offer, apart from the official commemoration of a past when the port really was still the point of departure for North Africa, the Lebanon, and Indo-China: huge white monuments, facing seawards from the main *corniche*, to the colonial troops and the marines.

The change has been so rapid that it is really quite difficult to recall that, as recently as the 1950s and the early 1960s, the huge, barrack-like, noisy hotels of the Cours Belsunce still witnessed a regular coming and going of tin trunks, proof against ants, rust, and the other multiple hazards of the African climate; trunks often of quite gigantic proportions, painted black, and with the names of the owners and the destinations—Oran, Tananarive, Sidi-bel-Abbès—painted on them in large white letters. Beside them were hatboxes containing green-lined, white pith helmets. Milling around were a baroque clientele of long-limbed Senegalese, their wives in lurid print frocks; venerable, bearded Arabs wearing

[1] Hero of a film directed by Julien Duvivier, 1937. 'Moko' is argot for Marseillais.

golden slippers; and harassed and screaming families of French officials returning to the *douanes indochinoises* or to duties in Madagascar or in Nouméa. Even the novelist Céline's ghastly crossing, as described in his famous *Voyage au bout de la nuit*—the crossing from Marseilles to Algiers—now seems a colonial period-piece, the polemics of which concern a shipload of ghosts.

Perhaps indeed all this is a type of 'homing' or of 'departing' literature which is likely, everywhere and in all languages, to see its days numbered, with the relentless shrinking of travel by sea and of the ready sociability and equally ready detestation—how important the seating at table assigned to one, the first night out, by the pur-ser, an entry to bliss, to purgatory, or to boredom—of *la traversée maritime*. For it would be beyond the scope of the most imaginative novelist to reconstruct a conversation, much less a 'plot', set in an aircraft, however long and tedious the flight.[1] If the 'passage out', from Liverpool or Southampton, to Bombay, had so long served as a preliminary marriage-mart to younger daughters of English middle-class families, in France, too, Marseilles must so often have been the predictable, indeed, looked-forward-to, point of depar-ture of a tentative exploration, ending perhaps, if all went well, in marriage to a *fonctionnaire colonial*, to an army doctor, or to an officer in the *tirailleurs algériens*. Such standard plots—so standard as not even to qualify for a literary description as *l'intrigue*, because the plot was provided in advance, was there to be acted out—in the regularly repeated, yet significant, even touching, *histoire des familles*, have always remained largely unrecorded in works of imagination as in history itself (both equally hostile to the in-vocation of an imperial past), being confined to the semi-private ar-chive of the devotedly kept family photograph album, itself an effort at groping reassurance, a bold and often pathetically inadequate claim on the uncertainties of a bottomless future (I can still recall being shown, while billeted with Polish officers in a small hotel next to the Pleasure Beach in Blackpool, in 1941, the albums of young lieutenants and sub-lieutenants, often their only visual links, apart from the odd *czapska* or the silver braid, rather frayed, sewn on to the collar, relics of uniforms that had survived many moves, with a past not at all distant in time—1938, 1939—but politically indescribably remote, even then—though none could then have known just *how* remote—processions and march-pasts,

---

[1] But see the excellent short story 'The Dull Man' by Noel Blakiston (*The Collec-ted Stories of Noel Blakiston*, London, 1977).

the white-red flags unfurled, the coloured chokers of youth organisations, the triangular caps, baroque churches, a flat country-side, squat cottages, whitewashed, with low thatched roofs, dramatic wells, armies of geese): '*voici Jacques en blanc*,' '*voici le commandant un tel, je ne retrouve pas son nom*,' '*voici le départ de Marseille; on voit Notre-Dame-de-la-Garde*,' '*voici la rade d'Alger*,' '*nous voici arrivés à Saïgon*,' '*voici la table du capitaine, c'est moi en smoking*,' as natural a frame for a novel of banality, habit, and reassurance, as the fixed itinerary imposed by the long, single street of Fontenay-le-Comte leading from the station, via the Sous-Préfecture, the Banque de France, eight cafés, seven *notaires*, four *huissiers*, la Banque Agricole de l'Ouest, two hotels facing one another from opposite sides of the street, the Café-Bar des Sportifs, the *parc municipal*, with a pond, an artificial island bearing a miniature *château-fort* and connected to the mainland by a Japanese bridge, the *gendarmerie nationale*, and *commissaire de police*, the Pompiers, a group of Indochinese passing in the direc-tion of the station, a group of nuns passing in the opposite direc-tion, to the cathedral and the château at the far end: Simenon's *Au Bout du rouleau*, the end of the line indeed, in its stark, French Primer predictability.

Each *escale* would offer a further stage in tentative exploration and emerging intimacy, the last night of the trip out, before land-ing, might represent an all-or-nothing risk, a desperate win-all or lose-all, which, in the former case, might result in inclusion in the photograph album, a measure of time that proceeds at a pace even more leisurely than that of the Messageries Maritimes or the Compagnie Paquet, but as predictable as the progress from port to port of a well regulated steamship line. One is reminded of the no doubt common experience of the *soldat deuxième classe* Valentin Bru, in Queneau's *Le Dimanche de la vie*, whose personal geography of France has been confined parsimoniously to his birth-place in a Paris suburb, to Marseilles, where he had embarked for Madagascar, to Bordeaux, where he had disembarked on his return, and to Le Bouscat, a suburb of Bordeaux which housed the barracks of a colonial depot.

It could be argued that most such passengers would have been too pressed for time, too worried about their luggage, too afflicted by the first attack of the *mal du pays* and by the onset of fear of the unknown, or too eager to reach without delay a beloved home town or village, its virtues greatly inflated in the exile of

Tananarive, Djibouti, Abidjan, Pointe-Noire, or Brazzaville, to
have taken in the cascading, steeply terraced, ochre-coloured city,
as glimpsed at a sudden bend of the railway line above L'Estaque,
or diminishing slowly, falling into itself, first the two forts, then the
dome of the cathedral, then the tiers of red-roofed houses, then the
Virgin, and finally even the brown and russet hills, before all disappeared in the sea, sternwards: all the more so because departure
and arrival would so often occur at unusual times, at first light, or
in the middle of the night, as if further to emphasise the apartness
of the maritime traveller and to separate him from the sleep of the
resident inhabitants, that other great barrier that divides the night-
worker from the sleeper. Yet how many times must such an impression have been indelibly marked on the retentive retina of personal or collective family memory! There can be no more dramatic,
more significant introduction to New York or to Cape Town than
that by sea; and a general view of Marseilles, perched on the edge
of its broken bowl, a huge amphitheatre open to seawards, must
thus have marked, like the shutter of a camera, the departures and
the arrivals of countless people, measuring out the regular course of
a career in colonial service, with intervals of leave, new postings,
gradual promotion, interrupted every now and then by
alcoholisation or the regular return of malaria, marked too,
possibly, by marriage, during one of these periods of leave,
following the placing of a carefully worded advertisement
—personal appearance, age, health, tastes, leisure habits, moral
qualities, present employment, and future prospects specified
—written out while in Abidjan or in Douala, in a specialised
paper, such as *Le Chasseur Français*, the dream literature of the
lonely colonial, a paper passed around, closely scrutinised, and
mulled over, *petite annonce* by *petite annonce*, so reassuring in the
sheer mediocrity of mutual expectation offered and in the modesty
of both those who inserted and those who, in small towns in
metropolitan France: Parthenay, Issoudun, Châteauroux, Saintes,
Laon, Semur, Marcq-en-Baroeuil, Hénin-Liétard, Culmont-
Chalindrey, Saint-Germain-des-Fossés, Lambesc, Pont-l'Évêque,
read these pleas for companionship, for a sharing of experience,
however uninspiring, these brief exercises in ideal double
biographies, a strange dialogue, paid for at so much the line, and so
allowing little room for poesy and fantasy, like small bits of paper,
curled into a bottle, and thrown into the sea, as if the long arm of
the B.H.V., the Belle-Jardinière, or the Enfants de la Chapelle had

managed to reach right out into the green fastnesses of river outposts on the Congo or forest clearings in the Côte d'Ivoire, the
faithful, banal *Chasseur* as much a familiar witness of provincial
ordinariness as *l'Almanach des P.T.T.*

Each return would bring with it a sharp, rather bitter, and
uneasy awareness of nationality—for Marseilles would still
represent a sort of France even for a Frenchman who still had ahead
of him a thousand kilometres of travel before reaching La Bassée or
Maubeuge, Mayenne or Concarneau—and an equally acute, and
much more disturbing realisation of change, after a long absence:
the fact that the *agents* and the *douaniers* on the quayside wore ties
and no longer had their tunics buttoned up to the collar, the fact
that boaters and panamas had given way to berets, hats, and caps,
that alpaca and tussore jackets in postman beige were beginning to
be assigned to a museum of memory designed to house an already
mythical Tartarin, that beards and pince-nez no longer designated
the schoolmaster, the savant, the chemist, and the taxidermist; all
visible and sharp reminders of having been overtaken by events that
one had not experienced, that one had read about in newspapers
months old, by subtle changes that one had not witnessed in their
slow progress, of having missed out on a whole area of collective
national experience. That *classe*, for instance *classe de 38*, those
young men who had remained with the colours, mobilised in the
French Army, under the terms of the Armistice of June 1940, and
who had, shortly after the formation of the Vichy Government,
been shipped off, via Marseilles, to North Africa, Syria, or
Madagascar, serving in colonial troops until the Liberation, must
have returned to a France bewilderingly unrecognisable, even in its
deep and bitter divisions, into which they could not readily be re-
accepted, for the simple crime of merely having been out of things
for four or five years; neither *collabos*, nor *résistants*, nor even
prudent *attentistes*, but absentees, involuntary deserters from a
testing-time of choice in national history, cut off both from the
humiliations of foreign occupation, the discomforts of the curfew
and of privation, and from the small pride of refusal to accept
defeat. Superficially, the language would appear the same, but
many words would have acquired a new, hidden significance, a
whole vocabulary that would serve to exclude the ghostly *revenant*.
An experience of national rejection that must, over a century
earlier, have been that of so many *demi-soldes*, so many *grognards*,
back from the Grand Duchy of Warsaw, the Kingdom of Holland,

from the Départements Réunis, and from the Illyrian Islands.

To such, Marseilles, *la porte du Midi*, the southern sentinel of *l'Hexagone*, might present the same appearance from far out to sea: the two forts at each side of the mouth of the old harbour, the mosque-like contours of the cathedral, a place apparently of Eastern worship and rite, the huge Virgin at the summit of Endoum, the beige, russet, and mauve hills, the brilliant white of the Château d'If, on its stony grey and green island, even the cranes of La Joliette, giving a deceptive appearance of habitual activity. But, once disembarked, the immense space left where the Vieux Port had been, the absence of the *pont transbordeur*, giving to the old harbour an air of incompleteness, would underline the enormity of change and the chasm that would separate them for ever from the recent experiences of the Marseillais, and from that, as it were in advance, of the rest of their compatriots. A port lives as much in the memory and observation—always far more acute, always conditioned to a greater awareness and sensitivity to the concreteness of matter, to the texture of stone and wood, to the warmth of a wall, suddenly crossed by a darting lizard, to the aromatic plants growing in old stonework—of its passengers, of those who take ship and who land, as in the more dormant, more routinal, lazier, less intense memory of its permanent, land-based inhabitants. But each would be aware of a totally different town, of an urban geography quite unknown to the other. The distance from the height of a deck to the quayside is almost insuperable in mental terms; and to the ship's passenger, the lit-up destinations on the front of the blue trolley-buses and trams represent names that are meaningless, however poetic and inviting in their vagueness and unattainability—Belle-de-Mai, La Madrague, Saint-Jean-du-Désert —the end of the line of journeys that will never be taken, of small green oases of plane-trees and shutters, a fountain in a quiet square, a green fence overtopped by lilac, the *tête de ligne* of a numbered line of urban transport, where the trolley-bus can rest its long arm, unhooked from the overhead wire, and its driver and *contrôleur* can pause for a cigarette and a conversation, on a seat under a tree with its bark peeling.[1] A terminus then that cannot even be

[1] Or one of the splendid blue trams, carrying the blue cross on a white background of the city's arms, of Marcel Pagnol's childhood, recalled in *Le Château de ma mère* (1958): '. . . et ce fut le départ pour la "gare de l'Est". Cette "gare" n'était rien d'autre que le terminus souterrain d'un tramway, et son nom même était une galéjade. L'est, en la circonstance, ce n'était pas la Chine, ni l'Asie-Mineure, ni même Toulon: c'était Aubagne, où s'arrêtaient modestement les rails de l'Est. . . .

imagined, save in the promise of its evocative name, but that, to the traveller out, to the soldier or the sailor on his way back to discomfort, boredom, and loneliness, must yet offer a poignant and tantalising mirage of domestic peace, daily routine, and the assurance that tomorrow will be like today: *la vie en pantoufles*, at the end of both. Even bitterer the contrast, and greater the gulf, to those who are sailing on the evening tide or at nightfall, and who cross the city by taxi, shut away from its population, at a time when the buses and trams are taking their packed shirt-sleeved and summer-frocked loads of people, at the end of the day's work, back to the suburbs, back to a *pastis*, a game of bowls, supper, and bed, and sleep, perhaps vaguely disturbed, or, on the contrary, even encouraged, by the muffled fog-horn of the ship about to leave. Most unbearable of all, the lights going on in the streets, then in a tall window, then in a mass of windows at different levels, conveying an intimacy, a sharing in the collective life of the city, as it settles down for the night, a sense of almost maternal protection, from which one is excluded, on the threshold of general sleep.

On the other hand, perhaps in an interval between hustling from the Gare Saint-Charles to the port of la Joliette, the transient, on his outward journey, might spend the night in a noisy, carpetless, stone-floored hotel in the Cours Belsunce or in the Quartier de la Bourse. But, in his flickering sleep, he would be drifting in a sort of geographical limbo or already ahead of himself physically, in a gently throbbing ship.

He might take a meal, or several meals, in a large restaurant facing on to the Vieux Port. On the other hand, he might take a meal in a deep narrow restaurant with an unassuming entrance facing on to the rue des Phocéens; and, like the chap opposite him, his *vis-à-vis*, he might order a *rosé de Provence* and fish soup, or, like the shopgirl or the country family opposite, he might have a plate of squids, *sèches à l'armoricaine*, or, like the old man at the next table, he might be reading the evening paper, in an effort, perhaps, to cling on to scraps of local news: a brawl, a burglary, a wedding, a *pétanque* match, a *vin d'honneur* (a presentation on nous sortîmes des entrailles de la terre, juste au début du boulevard Chave, à 300 mètres à peine de notre point de départ. . . .' A municipal itinerary no more discoverable by the stranger passing through than *le train bleu* from Lyons to the Île Barbe. But the discovery of such local lines of transport gives the more permanent visitor both *droit de cité* and a sense of belonging in a municipal community. *Le train d'Aubagne* is as much a password to Marseillais particularism as *le train d'Arpajon* (or, more familiarly, *l'Arpajonnais*)would have been to that of Paris before 1937, when the train was replaced by a bus.

retirement)—the everydayness and guaranteed renewability of a land-locked existence. He, the transient, is rather like a drowning sailor who clings on to a piece of floating wood; as if some minor *revolverisation* in the Quartier du Panier or an accident involving a trolley-bus and a scooter would actually put off the imminence of departure, granting him, as it were, a tiny bonus of 'territoriality'. He might then follow the conversations around him—indeed, he could hardly fail to do so—the pointed vowels as reassuringly local, fixed, and familiar as the violet-scrawled menu; and yet, despite such desperate exercises in immobility as his feet firmly set on the red-tiled floor, his elbow resting on the paper cloth, his nostrils taking in the aromatic smells coming from the kitchen, his eyes brushing over the busy, concentrated fraternity of the eaters, all engaged in the same rapid rites, his ears holding on to the fall of a sentence or to hurried greetings accompanied by a perfunctory handshake across the table—'*à demain*,' '*à dimanche*,' '*bon weekend*'—it is but a pathetic effort actually to lay hands on and to caress an immediate future totally inaccessible. Already, he is removed by thousands of mental kilometres from those sitting opposite him, those who might even have spoken to him as across an immense but invisible gulf, those who know the waitresses by name. And something of his apartness would be communicated to them, too. They would not be deceived by his close reading of the evening edition of *Le Provençal*.[1] The concentrated attention of the solitary eater to all that surrounded him—the arrival and departure of customers, the comings and goings in the busy, narrow street outside, the tour of the tables by a deaf-and-dumb man depositing at each place his printed biography: '*Je suis sourd-muet de naissance . . .*' (and coming back on his round to collect them again, most of them left unopened, sadly) or the tour of the tables by the lottery salesman—would reveal him for someone already on the brink, beyond the comforting embrace of habit, of a fixed itinerary, even of a tiny participation in a collective routine.

Or perhaps, because of living in a port, they would scarcely notice him at all; they would simply write him off almost as a non-person, as one already outside the visible perimeter of the regular

---

[1] Pagnol's mother has a more practical use for the blue-titled paper; Marcel and his friend Lili are going out into the hills in bitter winter weather: '. . . Elle nous habilla. Entre mon gilet de flanelle et ma chemise elle glissa plusieurs numéros du *Petit Provençal*, pliés en quatre. Elle en mit aussi dans mon dos. . . . Lili, bouleversé par ce désespoir, me prit dans ses bras, froissant entre ces coeurs désespérés seize épaisseurs du *Petit Provençal* . . .' (*Le Château de ma mère*).

eating-place, regular eating-time, and regular leisure.

The result of all this has been that such literature as concerns Marseilles has been written by strangers and by travellers on their way somewhere or other, whose only reason to be in the city would be to get out of it, and so only aware of the place as a point of rest or waiting, preferably brief, but always of uncertain and unwelcome duration. For Victor Serge, it is waiting for a visa to Mexico or somewhere else, a daily tour of consulates; for Arthur Koestler, the crowded febrile waiting-rooms of yet other consulates; for Airey Neave, a flat owned by a doctor, a member of a well-known local medical family, somewhere on one of the *corniches*, with a magnificent view seawards, that can never be extended or varied in any way—three dusty palms, a grey wall, a blue-and-white advertisement for Noilly-Prat, two islands out to sea, enclosed implacably in the frame of long-windows—because he cannot be allowed out, lest his accent or his appearance give him away, till means can be found to remove him by sea, from a nearby *calanque*, and transport him to Gibraltar; for Léon Blum and other Socialist deputies, a confusing wait, actually on board, on the *Massilia*, a ship that, in the end, never sails, as if reluctant to leave her home port, and part company with the city the name of which she carries; for Joseph Kessel, a *tournée de cafés*, not for pleasure or refreshment or for the enjoyment of company, but in search here of a liberating rubber-stamp, there of a ration card, here of a false identity card, there of a photographer, a tiring circular tour of specialised underground skills. All that Evelyn Waugh could retain of the place was the cheekiness of the prostitutes, as they leant out of windows to deprive his leading character of his hat—a ridiculous object—and the washing that hung from windows or, like brightcoloured bunting, on lines across the narrow streets. Few travellers, even French ones, seem to have been bothered to take in much more; and both French and foreigners appear, in their cursory glance, to have regarded the inhabitants of the port in much the same way as passengers through the Canal might have thought of the Egyptian salesmen as they swarmed around the ship or the quayside at Suez. All seem to have been remarkably uncurious about the inhabitants of the second city of France; in return, the resident Marseillais seem to have been principally concerned to hold travellers and strangers at arm's length and to maintain the sharp distinction between the city as a *lieu de passage* and as a place to live and work in.

During the First World War the city would witness the brief passage of British servicemen, travelling overland, to take ship here for the Dardanelles, and that of those fortunate enough to make the return trip. During the Second it would perhaps just discern the coming and going of successive garrison commanders and high-ranking officials to and from Syria. Only the massive exodus of the *pieds noirs* from Algeria on the eve of Independence seems strongly to have impinged on local awareness of such movements, whether regular or exceptional, while the port could absorb, in its in-difference, the constant comings and goings of patriarchal Algerians, carrying enormous bundles and accompanied, a few paces ahead, by small groups of veiled women, as they headed towards or away from the Gare Saint-Charles. And so, in general experience, it would be recalled as a place in which the *waiting* was above all demoralising, as a sort of twilight zone in careers spent in the colonies or in the colonial armies: a threshold, neither one thing nor another, neither quite the *métropole*, nor quite the African or Far Eastern shore, but suspended in a point of time and space be-tween the two, and so a time and place for uncomfortable self-awareness and self-examination, doubt, bewilderment, hope, and fear. Of such passers-through, there is no visible record, save perhaps in the well-worn steps of Saint-Charles,[1] though for those prepared to carry the search a stage further there might still exist at least the terse evidence of name and surname, several names and the same surname, the suggestion of a family on the move, nationality, passport number, whence coming and whither going—not that either would give away much—in the *fiches de police* filled in before a night's stay at a hotel: that so-and-so, claiming to have been travelling from Paris, had stayed one night, Cours Belsunce, before embarking for Algiers. It would be as if they had never existed other than as staccato paper biographies filled in hurriedly at a hotel desk and ending up in some indifferent section of the Prefecture. And, for soldiers and sailors, of whatever nationality, who were travelling collectively, there would not sub-sist even that derisory monument.

Pépé-le-Moko gazes with tears and bitter nostalgia through the iron railings fencing off the port of Algiers, because he is on the

---

[1] It was only those who stayed who might acquire a brief mention in local literature, as naturalised Marseillais: '. . . Joseph assimila son cas à celui d'un coif-feur berlinois, venu à Marseille pour trois jours, en mission syndicale, et qui n'en était jamais reparti . . .', an instance flattering to local reassurance (Marcel Pagnol, *Le Temps des secrets*).

wrong side of the Mediterranean, with his life-blood running out onto an unfamiliar *pavé*—because his dreadful, hopeless nostalgia has been exacerbated by listening to a few old records of Fréhel's songs, accompanied by Fréhel herself, a ruin of herself in a cracked alcoholic voice, and because the white ship, that he will not take, is heading for home, *his* home: Marseilles, now a distant and desirable city, never attainable. But Pépé is an expatriate Marseillais (though he is in fact Jean Gabin, a native of the Seine-et-Oise, almost a Parisian), an exile, now stranded on an alien shore, like the sad, dejected, hopeless, alcoholised poor whites left behind for ever in the port quarter of Cape Town: Swedes, Norwegians, West Germans, Dutchmen, Scots, stuck there, with no hope of escape, cadging drinks from any unfamiliar customer. Very few Marseillais of Marseilles would ever get near to understanding Pépé's agony; and perhaps the only inhabitants who might be able to cross that mental barrier would be the prostitutes who thicken in ever increasing clusters in the narrow streets approaching the Quai des Belges and the rue des Couteliers, as a last reminder that this was the traditional, historical approach to the city from the sea right up to the nineteenth century, before the construction of La Joliette, and one still reserved for visitors of state right up to the present century, the unfortunate Alexander of Jugoslavia, disembarking at the very foot of the Canebière, as if to save his assassins trouble and to be in ahead of time on his own murder, a few minutes after landing, a hundred yards or so further on.

By the nature of her profession, the prostitute will be in contact, above all, with transients. Even the gangling Bretonne or the massive Ardéchoise will represent the last physical link with *le pays*, so that *une passe*, in conditions however brief and breathless, takes on a much deeper significance, almost tender, maternal and lingering, long after physical contact has been broken. She will be in contact with a moving and primarily non-Marseillais population, men from every other area of France and from all of what had once constituted *la France d'outre-mer*—a momentarily complete racial integration—thus achieved in the queue spreading out into the street from the *hôtel de passe*.

Prostitutes are always the most reliable guides to the normal patterns of movement, outside those of work, within a city, and to the most commonly used points of entry to it and departure from it: a simple fact of urban social geography at one time illustrated in Paris, in telling simplicity, by the constantly crowded pavements

and the many red pompoms of the French Navy, of the rue du
Départ and the rue de l'Arrivée, on both sides of the old and
modestly provincial Gare du Montparnasse, and the equally naval
aspect of the rue du Havre, alongside the Gare Saint-Lazare, a
reminder also that the Bastille and the Porte de Vincennes, as well
as Austerlitz or the Gare de l'Est, are railway or bus termini, that
the Porte de Clignancourt stands opposite the Reuilly barracks,
that the now mostly demolished rue des Partants, in Ménilmontant,
once stood close to a barracks, also gone, and that it contained a
row of brothels, still recognisable as such by their blind outer walls
of washable cream-coloured brick and by their lack of ground-floor
windows, though they have long since been converted to serve
other purposes; a reminder that soldiers and sailors, like provincials—and most of them *are* provincials—have always regarded
Strasbourg-Saint-Denis and the adjoining streets, above all the rue
d'Aboukir and the rue Berger, as the true centre of the capital:
where *pleasure* is, *there* is the centre. But in Marseilles, such concentration of pleasure will actually turn its back, as if in disdain, on
the station, the Gare Saint-Charles, and will thicken from the level
of the Chamber of Commerce and its neighbour, the naval
headquarters, guarded by two sentries in white belts and white
spats, as well as from the level of the Bourse and the Comédie, and
acquire maximum intensity in the rue des Couteliers, behind the
Hôtel de Ville, a street long familiarised to the white kepis of the
Legion, to the long Sénégalais, to the tiny Indochinois, as well as,
briefly, to the G.I.s of the American base.

    How many *secrets d'oreiller*, secrets of the pillow, most of them
of no value whatsoever to the D.S.T., the French counter-
espionage, or to the Sûreté Nationale, poor little secrets, banal
tragedies, paltry inadequacies, mean, unimaginative little crimes
sighed or whispered hurriedly on the sweaty, coverless bolster, or
murmured while buttoning up, as the girl stands in front of the
mirror to fix her lurid mouth or crouches rather perfunctorily over
the bidet—a rapid gesture of orthodoxy rather than of hygiene, as if
the customer were trying to get a little more for his money than had
been bargained for, a sort of last-minute clutching at reassurance
and intimacy, threatened by the menacing call of ships, in a lilac-
papered and red-tile-floored bedroom on the third floor, flickering
from the coloured lights of neon signs: Hôtel des Amis (as if in
derision of the eight-minute lodger), Hôtel de la Côte d'Ivoire,
Hôtel de Pézenas, Hôtel d'Alger, Café-Bar de Casablanca, Hôtel

Miramar, Hôtel de Suez, Au Rendez-vous des Toulonnais, Hôtel de Nice, Hôtel de Sisteron, the blue, green, white, and red geography of several continents starting or ending from Marseilles, of a score of *sous-préfectures* and *chefs-lieux d'arrondissement* emptying onto the city their surplus population (perhaps even in homage to the commonest home-towns of the girls themselves)! Brief Lives indeed, so many of them shortly to be terminated, with no final chapter beyond this strictly limited, commercialised pause of an intimacy well beyond the reach of family memory. And so what a store then of metropolitan and transoceanic experience, of the minutiae of a social history well below the level of significant ambition—merely that humble one of *du galon*, an extra stripe, or a single one, or that, simpler still, to survive and to return—below that of any chronicled importance, even in an obscure regimental history, yet a wealth of human material stored, briefly at least, in the confused and crowded memory of tired street-walkers, as they relaxed, in couples or in threes, in a bar on the ground floor of their place of work, for a *menthe verte* or a *grenadine*, for a short respite to chat loudly with colleagues, between a series of *passes*—five minutes, eight minutes (*strictement chronométrées*, for profit is in speed)—gaudily dressed, frayed *dépôts d'archives humaines*, walking on abnormally high heels, each life not even afforded the tiny luxury of a Christian or even a nickname, not even identifiable in the simplest police terms, and so recollected, perhaps, in some exotic tattoo on the chest—because the customer would not even have had time to remove his shoes, much less to undress. He is only vaguely and unhelpfully individualized as a sweaty face, made out as a grimace, a *rictus*, as if already rehearsing for death, looking downwards, and inquiring, in a local accent or in a French jargon, '*D'où tu es donc?*', in a sudden gabble of words designed even to cross the barrier imposed by such formal and ready *tutoiement*. Little then to carry the female witness, momentarily pinned down on the sheetless bed—covered by some grubby washable material—beyond the *tu* and the *toi*, a pair of eyes, a face little more revealing than an actor's mask, with tattoos on the upper arm or on the forearm, the unhelpful uniformity of a khaki shirt or a sailor's blue-and-white striped undervest. And yet, with so little to go on, an impressionism so sparse and as pared down to essentials as the furniture of the room itself, sometimes, almost unaccountably, leaving behind long afterwards the lingering memory of a man who had lost his way, who was frightened of the darkness ahead, and who was clutching briefly, like a child, at such commercially offered femininity.

But prostitutes, of course, do not write novels; though, if they reach very great eminence, such as Manouche did, they may have novels written for them, or about them.[1] Nor do prostitutes write history, save, every now and then, in the staccato records of *la chronique judiciaire*, the crime column, or, as it were, *par personne interposée* and at several removes, in the devitalised language of a *commissaire de police* or his secretary, following a *revolverisation* or a stabbing, an act of sudden vengeance so often adding a definitive conclusion to the life of the potential narrator. She was a woman who had made a sort of living by going up and by coming down, by listening inattentively to mumbled *bribes de conversation*, snatches of conversation, falling from the partner in a hurried ceremony and competing with a multitude of sounds coming through the walls on each side, together with the banging of doors and the distinguishable noise of masculine and feminine footsteps along stone staircases and passages, each word falling into a deep well of confused murmur, with perfunctory intervals to wash down below, the turning of the taps, the angry shudder of the gurgling water in the pipes, as if designed to acclimatise already the customer, as he puts on his jacket and searches in his pockets for a cigarette, to the throb of a ship's engine. Her life of repetitive work ended, meriting, perhaps, a few lines in a local newspaper, with each sentence preceded by the word *encore*—*encore un crime du milieu*; *encore un drame de la jalousie*; *encore un règlement de comptes*—as if to deny the individuality and uniqueness of her death and her manner of death, a departure as discreet and as sparsely recorded as those, every few minutes, of her *pratiques*, as they hasten back to the loneliness of the functional and rather awful collectivity of ship, of regiment, and of barracks.

For such witnesses, the only recorded literature would be the weekly or monthly letter, written in mauve ink on lined sheets of notepaper bought by the sheet with a single envelope at the nearest *bureau de tabac*,[2] to a child regularly visited at great cost, in-

---

[1] See below, p. 122

[2] Perhaps like the paper Marcel chose, in order to impress his little friend Lili, but that, in the end, he did not use: '. . . j'allai au bureau de tabac, et j'achetai une très belle feuille de papier à lettres. Elle était ajourée en dentelle sur les bords, et décorée, en haut à gauche, par une hirondelle imprimée en relief, et qui tenait dans son bec un télégramme. L'enveloppe, épaisse et satinée, était encadrée par des myosotis . . .' (Marcel Pagnol, *Le Château de ma mère*).

convenience, and loss of precious working-time who had been put out to a wet nurse, *en nourrice*, somewhere in the countryside not too far away from Marseilles, but as far away as possible from the girl's native town or village.

Already in the 1930s, Marseilles seemed so irresistibly set up as a sort of national joke-shop that it would take the peculiar circumstances of the Occupation to provide the place with a literature of its own, although a literature written mainly by novelists and poets who were refugees from the north. Today, thanks to the development of the enormous new southern industrial complexes of Fos and l'Étang de Berre, the joke-shop image is dated and, rather mercifully, I think, *la galéjade*, for export northwards only, has gone the way of the once-thriving trade in dirty postcards. But this very complex, very hard-working, and rather austere city still has not quite managed to develop an indigenous literature representative of its apparently ready expansibility, its sociability—a sociability easily accessible, but in fact hardly extending beyond the café terrace or the bar and certainly never reaching back into the impenetrable secrecy of domesticity and of the family. Thus a very masculine form of sociability.

And I do not think an indigenous literature has ever grown up to express the innate pessimism and melancholy hidden behind so much verbiage. Perhaps the potential capacity for native literature has always been exhausted in advance—in speech, in the constant fount of conversation, in the rich and flowing delight of the spoken word.

The arts seem deliberately to have been expelled from the *cité phocéenne*, as the Marseillais like to describe their city, as a reminder of its Greek origins, to make more room for trade, industry, medicine, science, and technology, as a result of the division, in the course of the nineteenth century, of what is still called the University of Aix-Marseille, in order to concentrate on what the Marseillais would call *les choses sérieuses*—science, technology, engineering, and, above all, medicine.

This sense of cultural sterility is certainly confirmed further, visually, even to the most casual visitor, by the predominantly nineteenth-century, Second Empire, early Third Republic (both at their very worst) architecture of what, in fact, is the oldest town in France, making of the port the most profoundly nineteenth-century ensemble in the whole country. Indeed, it produces a sort of Third

Republic rococo which achieves its most luxuriantly leafy ugliness
in the Cours Castellane, the triumphal exit from the city eastwards
towards Toulon and the Italian frontier, and again, in the extraordinary luxuriant statuary of the museum and the park of the
Pharo.

Furthermore, apart from its only too apparent architectural
brashness and vulgarity, there is certainly nowhere in France where
people dress more loudly, and where women's print dresses are
more strident. The Canebière, in the evening or at the week-end,
resembles a rural fairground, with a predominance of canary
yellow, pinks, mauves, and acidulous greens.

But what most characterises this Mediterranean port is its
secrecy. The ready loquacity, the easy sociability, the old standard
jokes are really screens, put up to deceive the Parisian and the
visitor from the north and to exclude him from the reality of a sort
of embattled family neighbourliness. The result is that Marseilles
can be, for the stranger, an extraordinarily lonely city. It would
seem that, for generations, one of the principal concerns of the
Marseillais has been to keep themselves to themselves, even at the
price of putting out to the rest of France a commercialised standard
image on the basis of the *galéjade* and the picture postcard. A
genuinely Marseillais literature, *à l'usage des Marseillais*, might
give too much away, so better not to write it down. Or merely leave
it to an always revealing *chronique judiciaire* in one of the local
newspapers.

Or possibly the old capital of the *royaume du Midi* has never entirely adjusted itself to the discipline and severity of a standard
language, gradually imposed, through education and ambition,
military service, and the railways, especially the P.L.M., from the
north, leaving, as it were, the local *chose écrite* high and dry in a
linguistic wilderness, and devitalising the once thriving local,
patrician culture of an eighteenth-century academic Marseilles.
Unlike Paris, the very cosmopolitanism of the city seems also to
have helped to create something of a cultural vacuum, as each
generation of immigrants has succeeded in preserving their own
linguistic identities: the Catalan sailors from the orange boats, the
phanariot Greek merchants who helped to finance Greek cultural
revival and linguistic modernisation, successive waves of Genoese
and Corsican settlers, followed, between the wars and even since,
by Tunisians, Moroccans, Algerians, Congolese, Senegalese, Côte
d'Ivoiriens, and, more recently, *pieds noirs*, amounting to a

linguistic diversity even more pronounced than that of Belcour and Bab'l Oued. Perhaps too it has been the misfortune of Marseilles, from a literary point of view, to have come too late to have experienced a linguistic revival—or possibly, a recreation, *de toutes pièces*, such as occurred in the sister port of Barcelona, in the late-nineteenth century, that is, at a time when social and economic links with Paris were already too strong to be broken, and when the ladder of ambition pointed so insistently, in the phrase *la montée à Paris*, northwards, for it still to be possible to justify a readiness to stay put. It may also have been that the city's prodigious commercial destiny had something to do with this literary indigence. In the past, the city has produced many writers; but most of these, from the Abbé Expilly onwards, it exported northwards; and the fact that Rimbaud died in the Hôpital de la Conception seems to have been a matter of indifference to most Marseillais. After all, coming, on his last journey, from Djibouti, where else *would* he have landed? Marseilles was a point of disembarkation as inevitable for the poet turned slave-trader as for any French traveller from North Africa, the Middle East, and the East African coast.

If, for the majority of the Marseillais, there was any sparse consolation to be had, in the terrible conditions of food shortage, cold, and scarcity resulting from the circumstances of the Occupation in the Mediterranean Departments, it would no doubt have been in the fact that Paris was no longer so readily accessible,[1] separated as it was from the southern port by an internal frontier, and, indeed, in that it was no longer the capital of France. Vichy could only be a different matter, owing to its proximity to the border of the old *royaume du Midi*; and it was bound to be more receptive to southern grievances. It might be argued, at least in terms of long historical memory, that the strange interlude of *l'État Français*, an accidental hiatus in French public history, represented, at least by promoting both Lyons and Marseilles to the position of the two principal cities within the new bifurcated state, *la revanche du Midi*.[2]

[1] That Paris was still very far away indeed, both in physical and mental terms, even after the construction of the P.L.M. at the time of the Crimean War, is suggested by a passage in Pagnol referring to 1870: '. . . À cette époque, Paris était bien plus loin de Marseille que ne l'est aujourd'hui Moscou. Il y avait trois jours et trois nuits de voyage, une centaine d'arrêts dans les gars, et plus de cinquante tunnels . . .' (*Le Temps des secrets*).

[2] It would not be altogether fanciful to suggest that, already under the Third

A certain deliberate and rather touching parochialism is apparent even in a work of local history (part, however, of a general series of the history of the resistance movement in France during the Second World War, planned and published from Paris at a national level) such as that of a local historian, Pierre Guiral, *Occupation, Résistance et Libération*, a work in which no one is really entirely villainous (Carbone and Spirito are, but they are expendable because they are Corsican immigrants), a work in which the relations between the local *Vichyssois* and the various brands of local *résistants* always remain at least correct, if not always cordial. Certainly, no breach ever seems to have been irreparable, no channel of communications ever completely cut off, so that a telephone call across the city, or a meeting by appointment in some discreet restaurant could generally keep all sides informed about what the others were up to, and prevent matters from ever getting out of hand—that is, out of the control of the various acknowledged leaders of the local community, including the members of the clandestine Communist party. Indeed, probably the man the least well informed of what was going on during the Occupation years was the Prefect of the Bouches-du-Rhône! It is a picture both convincing and reassuring in its generally prudent, unheroic dimensions, and a picture that carries the very clear message: *Que ceci reste entre nous, arrangeons les choses entre nous*, a habit of ingrained 'municipalism' that must have owed a great deal to past history and to long and bitter experience of interference from Paris.

Yet, one would think, in Marseilles of all places, childhood must have represented a point of time particularly sunny and luminous, the perception of blinding light and of an almost visible heat, the darting green and yellow belly of a lizard among stonework, the ragged, diaphanous, and reddish *rascasses*, that peculiar Mediterranean fish, and the rainbow colours of squids in the fishermen's baskets, the blue-painted Catalan boats piled with oranges,

Republic, and again, under the Fourth, the *revanche du Midi* could take the form of the colonisation of the rest of France by southerners who climbed up the educational ladder and who, in doing so, often climbed northwards, giving to Norman schools southern headmasters and headmistresses, *inspecteurs d'académie* and *inspecteurs primaires*. The ascension of Pagnol's *tante Fifi* is characteristic of an ambition especially southern: ' . . . Depuis sa vingt-cinquième année, elle était la directrice d'une école supérieure: elle y régnait en despote et se donnait toute entière à sa mission qui était d'instruire, d'éduquer et de former de jeunes citoyennes vertueusement laïques. . . . Bref, c'était une femme de bien, ce qui ne l'empêchait pas d'être belle, et de sentir bon . . .' (ibid.).

in a city which, as an immense and stepped playground, spills downwards towards the old harbour and the little beaches, and, like some other southern city, perhaps Rome, peters out all at once on the edge of the desert, a wild, aromatic scrub, high above the deep inlets, the *calanques*, on the reddish cliffs between Marseilles and Port Miou that dominate the sea, the approaches to the harbour, the three white lighthouses, and the islands lying out, their outlines obscured in a heat mist.

The sea is there to be looked at—a changing spectacle, with several shades of drifting colour—as well as there to be smelt. It is very doubtful, I think, if any of the residents would ever make the standard tourist trip to the Château d'If, and there are very few hints of the proximity of a port in the quiet rue Saint-Sébastien or among the market gardens, the soap factories, and the olive oil distilleries of Saint-Louis, Saint-Julien, and Sainte-Julie.

There is surely some negative significance in the fact that, in the four volumes of his childhood memoirs, Pagnol never once mentions either la Joliette or the Vieux Port; and there is nothing to suggest that the bright-eyed, very observant child had ever seen a ship, while the sea is only glimpsed at a great distance, reflecting the midday glare of a superb sunset, from the heights of the rocky *pinèdes* above Aubagne. What is more, it is always an empty sea. Even more surprising, the child never seems to have encountered a sailor, or, if he had, he does not consider the fact worthy of mention. His visual world is entirely land-locked, often confined to the heartless stone courtyards of school and *lycée*, but extending to the enchanted heights or valleys of the blue and tawny hills. An uncle had been to Rio, had indeed died there. But that is almost the only reminder that the boy was growing up in a great port. His father is entirely shuttered in by the conventional ambitions of the proud, but closed, hierarchy of the *instituteurs*. The mauve ribbon of the *palmes académiques* that beckons him on in his devotion to primary education and correct spelling, republican rectitude and conventional anti-clericalism, contains no hint of colonialism, nor of a *France d'Outre Mer*. Mauve is not the colour of departure, and, far from being an *invitation au voyage*, it is an insistent one to stay put within the familiar, safe territory of the *académie* and the reassuring geography of a *société savante*. It is as much a stay-at-home colour as the green of the *mérite agricole*. And its award will be duly mentioned in *Le Petit Provençal*, along with success in *boules*. Pagnol, it is true, does mention, *en passant*, the presence in his *lycée* of one or two Algerian boys, of two or three Annamites, even of a Japanese; but he does not feel that such exoticism is worth commenting on.

Equally indicative is his lack of curiosity about the parental background of his schoolfriends at the *lycée*. Only many years later does he discover that the orphan Oliva, a scholarship boy like himself, had been brought up by his two elder brothers, the one a stonemason, the other a docker. 'De même je n'avais jamais soupçonné que le père de Zacharias possédait soixante navires. . . .'[1]

When he wants to impress the little peasant boy Lili, who has apparently never come down from the heights of the plateau into the city, with his urban lore, the itinerary is entirely land-locked: '. . . je lui racontais la ville: les magasins où l'on trouve de tout, les expositions de jouets à la Noël, les retraites aux flambeaux du 141me [*not*, be it noted, a colonial regiment] et la féerie de Magic-City, où j'étais monté sur les montagnes russes. . . .'

Very few land-locked Marseillais would ever actually have been on the quayside of the docks, unless they were dockers or employees of the Port Autonome, or unless, rarely, they had come to see off a relative; at best, their observation, from one of the *corniches*, or from the sea front at l'Estaque, might register the arrival of the mailboat from Corsica, Casablanca, or Algiers, merely as a reminder of the day of the week or the time of the day, an extra public clock set seaward, a reminder that it is time to go home or to keep an appointment, to buy a weekly, or to catch the bank, or that, much more impressive, of a liner or a troop-carrier from Saigon or Oran, outside the normal calendar, or the reminder of the month provided by a shipping company.

So *la littérature de l'escale* would offer little appeal to the resident Marseillais, any more than it would to the resident Havrais or to the inhabitants of any other French port, most of whom would be remarkably uncurious about what went on beyond the twin lighthouses at the mouth of their harbours and, indeed, within their sight. The novel of the sea, of *le grand passage*, of terrible storms, typhoons, and near-shipwreck, has always had a much greater attraction for those living well away from the coast and less familiar with the constantly changing surface of the sea and the ocean, and, above all, to the Parisian, who, though living in France's most important port, would scarcely be aware of the fact,

[1] *Le Temps des secrets.*

beyond taking in, every time he crossed the Pont des Arts, the flags of the Belgian and Dutch barges, clustering along the quays of the Left Bank, below the Monnaie, or, if walking by those beyond the Gare d'Austerlitz, the big English coasters, with their blue ensigns, of the regular service Paris-Londres. To look seawards would not suggest any awareness of the significance of maritime matters; and the skyline of the steep city, climbing around its semi-circular bowl, in tiers of ochre-coloured red-roofed houses, their long green raffia blinds cracking in the wind from the hills, would not affect the inhabitants of the port in the poignant way it might the sea-borne traveller. There was no special wealth in a landscape that one could see the next day and the day after that. Notre-Dame-de-la-Garde and the Virgin of Endoum were unlikely to move overnight; and their special care was to watch over the departing or returning mariner rather than over those who lived in their shadow. The barrier between a land-locked literature and landed itineraries, and a literature that looks seawards, or that, from the other side of several seas, longs for land, will remain uncrossable.

As far as I know, apart from Pagnol's luminous memoirs, there has been no Marseillais equivalent of Henri Béraud, and no such childhood has ever been evoked in a novel or in recollections, and only once in a film, *Merlusse*,[1] mostly concerned with the eccentricities of a warm-hearted *maître d'internat*, an usher, and with the *internes*, the boarders, in one of the big *lycées*—the Lycée Thiers or the Lycée Saint-Charles—all living in an enclosed world of barrack-like discipline, Merlusse in his own peculiar tent in the middle of the dormitory, and all of them either strangers to the city or cut off from it.

Nor could one turn to the unhappy Germaine Roussier for as much as a hint of the physical awareness of her urban surroun-much as a hint of the physical awareness of her urban surroundings, of the port, its bright colours and its pungent smells. For impossible love for a teenage pupil and of a purely thematic, bookish education as a *professeur de lettres*, for whom literary characters possessed a reality denied to living people, and intellectual and theoretical discussion about generalities would obscure even a vague perception of what people might be saying around her; she was already as much a prisoner of her education and of her total intransigence while still living in freedom in a flat overlooking the port, as when, later, she was confined to the real

[1] Written and directed by Marcel Pagnol, 1935.

physical prison of les Baumettes; and one wonders whether she would even have been conscious of the change of scene. How could she have sought consolation or derived joy in the appearance of a town that she never *saw*, that she was incapable of seeing, living as she did in a barred and shuttered barracks of committed left-wing totalitarianism? The *affaire Roussier*, as its title implies, was not just another French dispute over the nature and the course of justice; it was also a polemic, an argument, an intellectual debate between people more concerned with ideology than with experience and observation. It offers no window on the town in which it took place, nor on its family life, all the leading participants being equally wrapped in the blindness of political fanaticism. So one cannot blame well-established Marseillais for expressing resentment at the publicity given to a human tragedy of starkly classical proportions merely because it occurred in a place of which most concerned seem to have been quite unaware. The *affaire* had nothing at all to do with Marseilles, save that, owing to the bureaucratic decision that sent the impossible young woman as a *fonctionnaire* to one of the *lycées* of the town, it happened, or mostly happened, in or around the port. Marseilles was merely a cardboard backdrop to Germaine's impossibilist fantasies; and, in any case, in most French provincial towns, the younger teaching personnel, coming mostly from outside, huddle together, like colonists cut off from their surroundings. Mlle Roussier is no more capable of witnessing, out of the depth of her myopic self-pity and total intransigence, for Marseilles, than would Jean-Paul Sartre, in his Parisian arrogance, and from the depth of *his* loathing for common humanity, have been able to witness for the inhabitants of Le Havre, the place to which he was sent for his first post and on which he attempted to avenge himself in *La Nausée*. It would be rather like asking Simone Weil to describe the wartime London in which she died. If the *affaire Roussier* has a lesson, from the literary point of view, it is that totalitarianism, whether of the Right or the Left, shutters the eye of the observer to anything outside that does not conform to an ordered, preconceived harmony, to the long dreary avenues, the squat, square mausoleums, the ice-cream blocks of Palaces of Culture, and the vast squares set aside for organised popular rejoicings; for the committed will only see with the regimented eye of a Le Corbusier, the perpetrator of *la maison du fada*, a blot on the Marseillais horizon, and the object of much popular derision. Germaine then can tell us nothing at all about the children of Marseilles, nor about the inhabitants in general, living as she did in the isolation of utter fanaticism, and killing herself when a glimpse of reality at last impinged on her atrophied awareness.

Apart from Henri Queffélec's *Journal d'un salaud*, a wicked incursion into the local family network of *la bourgeoisie marseillaise*, family, like childhood in the Mediterranean city, has remained inviolable, an object of mystery, save once more in a film, this time one made in the 1960s, *La Vieille Dame Indigne*,[1] a charming, perceptive, and compassionate account of the sudden revolt and liberation of an elderly widow previously caged in by the greedy, self-interested, and constantly watchful solicitude of her two sons and her two daughters-in-law, with grandchildren brought in as scouts, outriders, and informers. Set somewhere in the eastern suburbs, among the scattered red-roofed villas and *bicoques*, in the general direction of Aubagne, it is a very happy and sunny story which allows the old lady, trotting with her young protégée from Prisunic to Marché Leclerc, from *corniche* restaurant to shady *terrasse de café*, a very good run for her money. Indeed, she is able to get rid of most of it by the time she has given her family the slip for good by dying.

The *galéjade* was for northern consumption, an *attrape-touriste* to keep the Parisian and the northerner happy, even to give him the nudging impression of being in the know, of being admitted into the closed world of elaborate private jokes, while the Marseillais went about their business. For evidence of the survival of an indigenous popular culture and of a popular speech, one would have to turn from literature to the *chronique locale*, especially in the bitterly cold, windy winter months approaching Christmas, when the eloquent street vendors from the foothills inland lay out the brightly painted figurines of the crèches: Provençal shepherds and *vignerons*, fishermen, Arlésiennes, lavender-women from Grasse, Niçoises with their flat black hats and dark blouses, chestnut-vendors, and sellers of clay pipes, on the wide avenue climbing towards the ugly mass of the Église des Réformés. It is perhaps typical of the quirks and deformations of the Parisian view of things, of Parisian assumptions on the subject of the inhabitants of two cities that are still capable, even *now*, of getting along without Paris, even—ô *crime atroce!*—of ignoring Paris, of turning their

[1] Directed by René Allio, 1965.

backs on the capital and of looking southwards or eastwards, along axes of communication that do not include the city of the north—it is typical of Parisian myopia that it should be the Lyonnais who are traditionally depicted as secretive, closed-in, inhospitable, and jealous, and the Marseillais who are represented with their mouths wide open and their secrets pouring out.

Of course, there was a great deal more to such Parisian attitudes towards Marseilles than what one might call 'the profession-alisation of *la galéjade*' and a whole encyclopaedia of tried and very repetitive commercial-traveller jokes. There were the right-wing *nervis*—trigger men, gangsters, the Corsican protectors, includ-ing that irresistible duo of Carbone and Spirito, hiding under ex-ceedingly hilarious surnames the exceedingly nasty reality of many gangland killings in the Quartier du Panier, the underworld quarter of Marseilles, and other places never too far away from the waterfront, and, later, torturers and murderers in the service of the French Gestapo in Paris.

Certainly, Carbone and Spirito were not a very presentable pair, wearing long, belted mackintoshes and pigeon-grey *chapeaux taupés*—velour hats. Certainly, they always had stubbly chins. Cer-tainly, they were not devoid of a certain bandit chivalry: they gave lovely presents to Manouche, the protégée of Spirito and the sub-ject of an extremely amusing biography-cum-novel by Roger Peyrefitte. But they were certainly not comedians—unless one thinks that Carbone's death, his legs blown off by a mine set by the Resistance at the side of the main line between Marseilles and Dijon, is something which is good for a laugh.

An attitude of discretion in the presence of strangers, especially those from the north, can be readily discerned in Marseillais reac-tions to the very touchy subject of the city's changing, but generally thriving underworld. Most inhabitants would argue, rather fiercely, that the city was and is no more criminally inclined than any other great cosmopolitan port of its size and diversity, and it is, after all, a clearing-house for the whole of the Mediterranean, the Near East, and Algeria. In fact, they would argue, it was and is quite as safe as other French cities, and crimes of violence remain restricted to the professionals, the *gens du milieu*, but that Mar-seilles has always suffered from undue publicity in the national press as France's capital of crime.

Yet, at the same time, in a spirit of proud localism, the very same people would expatiate, rather knowingly, on the subject of what went on in the Quartier du Panier and would refer, with a touch of affection, to the multiple activities of the old *clan Guérini*, before it was finally broken up as a result of a series of murders, most of them committed in the rocky, hilly outskirts, and as a result of the defection of some leading members of the gang. [1]

The Guérini at least, though of Corsican or Genoese origin, clearly enjoyed *droit de cité*, the reward of long residence, complete integration, local intermarriage, and extensive charity, including the interests of the local football club, and a very touching respect for local interests and local hierarchies. They very much formed a well-established part of an oral literature on the theme of *Les Mystères de Marseille*, a sort of twentieth-century chap-book, a *livre bleu*, reserved exclusively to local story-tellers. [2]

But any interference from Paris was liable to provoke a stonewall of silence or even positive impediment, both reactions dramatically illustrated by the attitude of Sébeille, a local police inspector and a native of the port who, as a consequence, became something of a local hero, at the time of the prolonged enquiries into the Drummond murders in 1952. Lurs was well within the province of the Marseilles-based *police judiciaire*, and the presence of Parisian inspectors, and a highly critical corps of Paris correspondents was deeply resented, as a further example of Parisian meddlesomeness and interference. It is thus not difficult to understand why Simenon, a very discerning man, although a northerner, should never have risked the flair and experience of Maigret in these unpromising waters. It is rather as if he had decided that l'inspecteur Maigret, though he had been launched on London, New York, Geneva, and Lausanne, would never have been given any chance to make even the slightest progress in Marseilles. Maigret, who certainly is no stranger to the Côte d'Azur—after all, he has been to Antibes, Nice, Juan-les-Pins, Porquerolles, where he even sought very improbable excuses to prolong a quite blissful stay—has always given Marseilles a miss.

[1] There is an excellent section on the Guérini clan and on the traditional *milieu* of Marseilles in Lucien Bodard, *Les Plaisirs de l'Hexagone*, Paris, 1971, 'Néant à Marseille', 280-334.

[2] Something of this inbred provincialism is indicated by the social ascension, from lover to lover, of Bouzigue's sister, in Pagnol's account: '. . . un chef de dépôt des tramways, puis . . . un papetier de la rue de Rome, puis . . . un fleuriste de la Canebière, qui était conseiller municipal, puis enfin . . . le conseiller général. . . .' She was moving *upwards* alright, but within a purely Marseillais framework. (*Le Temps des secrets*.)

Nor has any other detective-writer in French pitted his talents against such an apparently recalcitrant and taciturn milieu. The French detective-story writer Exbrayat, in a whole series of *romans policiers*, has made, on the contrary, most effective use of the topography, the speech, the accent, and the cuisine of Lyons, and the familiarity displayed with all four is entirely convincing; but there is no equivalent for Marseilles, even at this harmless level of light entertainment. Yet, in the last few years, according to the detailed investigations carried out by *Le Progrès*, the local newspaper, Lyons would appear to have overtaken Marseilles as a European centre of crime, profiting from its proximity to Geneva and from its accessibility from Paris and Dijon. This has not prevented Lyons from retaining its own school of detective-story writers and of semi-professional criminologists, the successors of the famous Locard and Lacassagne, criminologists of the 1920s, and what, I think, is probably the finest *musée du crime* in the whole of Western Europe.

If a Marseillais were to object that Pagnol may have got things wrong, may indeed have fabricated caricatures for sale on a national market, the Parisian would probably shrug off his objections as ill-informed or, possibly, as inspired by some ticklish local conceit, just as the Parisian would take a great deal of persuading to accept the fact that Marseilles liberated itself in 1944 with only a minimum of American help, because it would be an article of faith with him that it was Paris and Paris alone which had succeeded in such an achievement. And so, if a group of Oustacha gunmen chose Marseilles as a base in which to assassinate, in 1934, Alexander of Jugoslavia, if Carbone and Spirito first emerged on the national scene in the port, and if Germaine Roussier opted for Marseilles as the place for her suicide, the Marseillais, in each instance, were in some way to blame.

I myself early acquired a view of France tempered by what might be described as *une mentalité 75* (though, before the War, Paris had a letter, or a series of letters, rather than a number, the initial letter always being an R—for *rassurant?*—as can be ascertained from any film by René Clair on the 1930s). Soon I could only see France through borrowed Parisian blinkers, for, save for a memorable visit to Rouen, regular week-ends at Samois (here one woke to the gentle chug of the French and Belgian barges, as the house was right on the river, within sight of the Pont des Valvins), and several summer visits to the village of Saint-Germain-de-la-Coudre, on the edge of the Orne and the Sarthe, and reached either on foot from the main line of the État, or by Citroën bus from La Ferté-Bernard, a village in which the children were extraordinarily polite and still wore clogs, Paris represented the totality of my geographical experience.

I have dwelt, at considerable length, on the Parisian view of Marseilles and its inhabitants, at least in the present century, because I believe it is quite fundamental to any understanding of Parisian assumptions about provincial France in general, and the Midi and the south-east in particular. I think it would be very interesting to take such an inquiry back into the previous century, as a further exploration of a very long background of misunderstanding, conditioning the mental blockage that has so much to do with the emergence at the level of Parisian awareness of what Parisians would call *le problème du Midi*, the problem of the south: a problem which is often of northern creation and, certainly, one of which most southerners are not aware, for I have never heard, in the Midi, any reference to the *problème du Midi*.

At the time of the Second Restoration, in 1815, the Prefect of the Bouches-du-Rhône and the garrison commander of Marseilles, both of them from the north, commented with rather condescending amusement, as if they were describing a tribal dance, on the childlike joy of the inhabitants of Marseilles as expressed at a great public festival held on one of the *cours* for the fête of Saint Louis. Of course, they went on in their enthusiastic report, they were well aware of the traditional attachment of the ever loyal Midi to the legitimate dynasty of the Bourbons, and did not need reminding of the terrible sufferings that the inhabitants of the port and of its wild hinterland had undergone during the dreadful years of the revolutionary wars. They further declared themselves deeply moved by such spontaneous manifestations of popular devotion to the Bourbon house: the women wearing their gayest colours and carrying green, white, or red silk parasols and pretty baskets of flowers; the fishermen dressed in their narrow jackets, wide blue velvet trousers, and dark hats covered in oilcloth; the children holding hoops and hobby-horses or pulling wheeled toys, clothed in striped waistcoats and brightly coloured frocks; the dancing of endlessly energetic farandoles; the whole vast concourse revolving hand-in-hand and facing inwards in ever widening or suddenly narrowing circles, to the sound of the fiddle, the flute, the *vielle*, and the shepherd's pipe, '*tout un peuple joyeux et en liesse*'; the huge white flags waving merrily in the sea-wind, while shouting boatloads of seamen and fishermen in long galleys, and armed with poles, jousted offshore, at the far end of the Canebière, in the old harbour. A splendid occasion indeed, and rendered all the more memorable by the presence of the duc d'Angoulême himself, the husband of the only surviving child of Louis XVI, the lieutenant-general of the faithful Midi, and the hero of ultra-royalism.

Yet, underlying the comments of the prefect and of the garrison commander, comments voiced *en style dithyrambique*, in inflated official prose, is the unstated assumption that the Marseillais are not to be taken entirely seriously, even in their perfectly genuine expression of joy at a great political change, long awaited, that had brought them immediate advantage and honour and the prom-ise of many more advantages and many more honours. They were regarded as being like little children: enthusiastic *tout en surface*, naïve, changeable, and unreliable. And also like children, their moods could easily darken from *allégresse* and song to cries for vengeance and acts of bloody violence, so that a farandole, begun in light-hearted good spirits, could easily degenerate into a series of lynchings. They were quite unpredictable, not to be trusted, blown this way and that by the contrary winds off the sea or off the chilly mountains of the Luberon; at one moment, full of courage and *plein d'élan*, at the next, running away like cowards. They were shallow, mendacious, boastful, unindustrious, content to bask in a prevailing sunshine and giving little thought to the morrow. In fact, they were some short of colonial people, childlike yet cunning, largely immune to sober reason and judgement, incapable of prolonged effort, readily bought offf by some highly coloured trinket or gay bauble that would match their brilliantly coloured clothes.

What they did not add, but what they no doubt thought, and what many of their predecessors from the north, and from the west, from Thibaudeau onwards, had both thought and, in fact, stated, was that they were little better than Hottentots and Zulus, which, of course, to the Parisian or to the northerner was hardly sur-prising, since they faced on to the African shore and turned their backs on what they would describe as *la civilité septentrionale*.

The attitude of these two officials echoes that of the novelist and Paris imperialist, Restif de la Bretonne, a great and enthusiastic convert to *le bon ton Parisien*, who, when all at once confronted with the horrible sights and sounds of the September massacres of 1792, had no difficulty at all in consoling himself with the comfortable reflection—on the subject of those who would go down in French history as *les septembriseurs*, members of the massacring mob, many of whom he had heard roaring through the streets of the Left Bank between 3 and 4 in the morning—with the comment, '*Aucun n'avait l'accent du parisis.*'

10

Paris *Xme*

There is always some danger, I think, both in historical terms and in those of literary localism, of confusing regionalism with provincialism, or even with what I would describe as a pseudo-peasant folklore. Those who react most strongly against the narrowness, the deliberate archaism, and the politically motivated reactionary romanticism of a Charles Péguy or of a Jean Giono—you know the sort of thing: the ancient rural values, a happy and unquestioning paternalism, the idealisation of *le labeur* by those who have never put their hands to a plough—will identify such a tradition with appeals both against Paris and against the political system established in Paris.

That sort of regionalism can very often be equated with antiparliamentarianism, and can best be located in just those areas of France in which an aristocratic nostalgia has, to some extent, survived—for instance, in La Varende's Lower Normandy, in the Bessin, the country round Bayeux; and in Michel de Saint-Pierre's west of France, as illustrated in his *Les Aristocrates*, and so on.

But there is also an abundant literature of Paris that, very far from being in any way national, is as firmly set in a local context as Jean-Louis Bory's celebrated semi-autobiographical book, *Mon Village à l'heure allemande*. To look at what appears to be a conflict between Paris and the rest of France in the perspective, for instance, of a very celebrated polemical piece that came out in the late 1940s—*Paris et le désert français*—is merely to equate Paris with a rather faceless authority, with Bureaucracy, and to forget that Paris is itself a whole jumble of quarters and villages, each retaining a very strong sense of identity, even though this is now tending to be lost, each existing in its own right as the framework for childhood, wonder, and exploration.

No literature, in fact, could be more pronouncedly regional than that of Paris and its neighbourhood. And while Léo Larguier's book, *Saint-Germain-des-Prés, mon village*, written in the 1930s, would now appear merely pathetic, as a reminder from a very, very long time back of an innocence and spontaneity long since lost, there is still plenty of life left for the evocation of this or that *arron-dissement*, this or that *commune* of the *grande banlieue*. Indeed, Georges Simenon has shown, with great skill, how such a theme as this sudden loss of identity, in personal terms, could still be hand-led, in his novel *Le Déménagement*—the move from Central Paris, from the Marais, to Cachan or Bagneux or Sarcelles or somewhere else farther out, south of Paris on the electric line, *la ligne de Sceaux*: a sociological fact that could be reproduced by thousands and thousands of similar examples.

Even *gauchisme* can readily accommodate the diversity of Parisian geography, and May 1968 was, above all, a phenomenon confined to a couple of *arrondissements*—the *Vme* and the *VIme*, on the Left Bank. And it was a phenomenon that brought few enough echoes on the Right Bank, even if many of the most active participants, after revolutionising all day, were, most nights, in the habit of returning to their homes in the *XVIme* and *XVIIme arron-dissements*, to sleep it off.

Nor could anyone be more provincial and more élitist than *les mandarins*, as described in the memoirs of Simone de Beauvoir: very self-satisfied intellectuals who move in a very narrow physical and social circle. Indeed, they are not all that different from the two *normaliens*, Jallez and Jerphanion, as described in the immense novel *Les Hommes de bonne volonté* of Jules Romains, and from all those who observe the sleeping city from the roof of the rue d'Ulm, which is the street which houses the École Normale Supérieure.

Certainly, *I* have not forgotten Paris, nor its suburbs. I have omitted them so far because I have been speaking mostly of exiles writing in Paris, and writing with the added nostalgia of absence, lost innocence, and death. How, indeed, could one forget such wealth and diversity as are provided by the tumultuous Paris of childhood?—the sunny, silent, empty Paris of June 1940, the Oc-cupied Paris of the ration cards, of the J3, and of the black market, the Front Populaire of 1936, recalled in the suburbs, Villeneuve-Saint-Georges during the Occupation years, in René Fallet's first novel *Banlieue sud-est*; *Les Enfants d'Aubervilliers*, the title of a very remarkable documentary film of the 1930s about sad, rickety, tubercular children; Charles-Louis Philippe's description of the Quartier de la Gaîté, behind the old Montparnasse station, in his novel *Bubu*; the mediocrity and the small-mindedness of the Passage des Panoramas, which is where Louis-Ferdinand Céline,

Dr. Destouches, spent his own rather unhappy childhood and which he exploited both in *Voyage au bout de la nuit* and in *Mort à crédit*.

Paris, on the contrary, must dominate any attempt to explore varieties of regionalism through works of imagination, as indeed it should, for, of all the infinite forms of French and francophone regionalism, that of Paris is the most insistent, imperious, the most cantankerous, the funniest, and, certainly, always the most inventive.

I am very conscious of this and, in my own case, of the strength of my own affiliations, experiences, mishaps, and near disasters, sudden glimpses of absolute happiness, like an April Paris shaft of sunlight all at once lighting up a leprous wall at the top of a house, cut down the side, like a chunk of ice-cream, Utrillo-coloured, and making it appear warm yellow. I remember the surrealist quality of so many Parisian itineraries: Filles-du-Calvaire to Barbès-Rochechouart; Sèvres-Babylone to Marcadet-Poissonnière; Corentin-Cariou to Corentin-Celton; Château-Rouge to Glacière; Strasbourg-Saint-Denis to Richelieu-Drouot; Château-d'Eau to Levallois; Porte-Brancion to Porte des Lilas; Robespierre to Jasmin; La Motte-Picquet-Grenelle to Sully-Morland; De Gaulle to Convention. I remember, too, the *Métro aérien* on green, raised bridges, clanging along at the level of fourth or sixth storey, opening up façades and giving a sort of running view of a bedroom, a kitchen, a dining-room, the figures silhouetted in activity; *Métro à éclipses* suddenly coming out into the light and just as soon disappearing once more into the semi-darkness of tunnel. And I am old enough to have travelled by tram down the boulevard Saint-Michel in the direction of the Gare de l'Est (and that certainly does date me), and I have, indeed, been so much conditioned by Paris—much more than by any other place, even Ixelles—that I feel it really necessary to place on record my own early subjection to Parisian imperialism.

Whether it is an advantage or a disadvantage I would hesitate to say, but I think there is certainly very much to be said for beginning with the capital of a country, provided one gets round the rest of the country at some later date. In my case, my first exposure to France, its language, its population, its climate, its sudden and terribly alien gusts of violence, and its reassuringly regular movements of work and leisure, of the week and the week-end, the differentiation of class as judged by clothing, came to me in the form of Paris.

My first introduction to Paris was not to the fashionable parts of the city; it was to the *Xme arrondissement*, just where it borders on the *IXme*, as well as where it borders on the busy Quartier du Sentier, the not very reputable rue de la Lune, a steep walk up to vice, almost as steep, but certainly not so long as the climb up to redemption, provided at the top by the hideous Sacré-Coeur, and the ancient theatreland of the boulevard Saint-Martin.

To the north lay a whole maze of *passages*, undetected even by Céline or by Aragon, and so lost to literature. Immediately below the boulevard Bonne-Nouvelle, where I lived, ran a sort of gully that on the day of the execution of Louis XVI, in January 1793, had provided the royalist conspirator, Baron de Batz, with a platform and, as he had hoped, literally a jumping-off ground from which to storm the heavily guarded *berline*, the carriage containing the king and his Irish non-juror confessor, l'Abbé Edgeworth.

To the right, a leaden January sky was brightened by the huge black-and-red pennant that flew over the offices of the newspaper *Le Matin*, and by the enormous, apparently fortified Rex, the largest cinema in Paris, a sort of vast, rectangular cube in beige cement that looked like a permanent ice-cream.

Beyond the Rex and beyond *Le Matin* were the salerooms and the offices of auctioneers of the *commissaires-priseurs*, the official valuers, of the Hôtel des Ventes, of the rue Drouot, and their offices in the neighbouring rue Rossini and in the Cité de Trévise, which is partly closed in with glass passages. And there was a female population certainly representative of every province of France and, indeed, pretty well the whole French empire, as well as of francophone Belgium and of Luxembourg, as one approached the Folies-Bergère via the rue du Faubourg Montmartre.

It was an area of central Paris that had been a *quartier d'agrément* in the time of Baron Haussmann, in the Second Empire, because it was in such convenient proximity to the Bourse, to the Sentier, to the newspaper offices, and to all the theatres of the *grands boulevards*. But, well before 1914, it became an area that was going into a steady social decline. As early as 1900, affluent and middle-class *boursicotiers* and *agents de change*, stockbrokers and so on, and currency speculators had begun moving out from the tall apartment buildings and migrating towards the more fashionable area to the west.

And so at No 26 boulevard Bonne-Nouvelle, where I lived, the impressive double doors to the flats on the first, second, third, and fourth storeys bore the names of Polish furriers and tailors, of private detective agencies, of doctors, though probably not very good doctors—doctors who played safe by specialising in *la sécurité sociale* and *les accidents de travail*.

From my bedroom window I could hear both the dull rumble of the Métro, which is very shallow at this point, and the continuous clatter of machinery that sounded as if it might be related to the activities of the Armenian *tapissiers* whom, in a voyage of discovery from fifth to seventh floor, I found to be established towards the top of the house.

The terrible screams and apparent cries for help that had so alarmed me during my first week, inducing me to believe that Paris was undergoing a replay of the September massacres next door to my bedroom and laid on specially for my benefit, were eventually traced to the presence, on the bottom three floors of the building immediately to the west, of the public baths the Bains Neptuna.

Immediately below the flat, the pavement widened out so as to include several *kiosques* with elaborate ironwork turrets, selling the newspapers of the world of the 1930s, including *Pravda*, *Izvestia*, and papers from Prague, Warsaw, and so on. At week-ends and on public holidays, there were street bands—one or two concertinas, a drum, and a very hoarse singer—selling sheet music of the latest hits.

On Saturdays and Sundays, the very wide *chaussées* were invaded by lugubrious family processions and by noisy, catcalling young men and by girls who had come in from the factory suburbs to the north and the north-east of the city, who were sufficiently ill-informed about the more recent shifts in Parisian fashions to believe that the Porte Saint-Denis and the Porte Saint-Martin and the *grands boulevards*, from there to Richelieu-Drouot, still constituted the very centre of the capital, the place where all the important things happened and where all the great shops had their frontages.

During the week, the crowds walked fast and humbly, bent down to face the east wind that swept in from the direction of the République. Haussmann, thanks to his east-west grid, succeeded in rendering Paris one of the coldest cities in Western Europe. And when I came to know the Left Bank better, I could appreciate that the area around the Métro station Glacière had earned its name doubly.

Crowds poured out of the shallow station Bonne-Nouvelle and

headed for the Bourse, the Sentier, the rue Turbigo, the rue Drouot, the newspaper and printing offices of the rue Réaumur, the big shops, the chain restaurants and cafés of the boulevards themselves: *petits employés*, clerks, waiters, shop assistants, tailors, seamstresses, printers, *commissionnaires*, errand boys, armed in the mornings of the 1930s with such papers as *Le Petit Parisien*, *Le Journal*, or *Le Matin*, and armed in the evening with *Paris-Soir* or *L'Intransigeant*. I really never discovered anybody who read *Paris-Midi*, a midday or afternoon paper, apart from those bent either on attending the afternoon races at Vincennes or at Longchamps or on betting on them at the betting-shop, the Pari Mutuel Urbain.

It was an area of what you might call *grand passage*, of work and leisure, a little too far to the east to attract the tourists, whether foreign or provincial, and too far from the Left Bank, from the Palais Bourbon, from the Place de la Concorde, the ministries, the embassies, or any of the railway termini, ever to attract a political demonstration or procession. Left-wing processions and demonstrations tended to pack up at the level of the République as their farthest point west. Right-wing demonstrations or processions favoured the boulevard Saint-Michel or the prestigious Champs-Elysées, so that the *Xme arrondissement*, whether by luck or negligence, or as the result of important matters having increasingly tended to pass it by, had consequently fallen into a sort of political apathy.

The family with whom I was staying were survivors from a more prosperous and prestigious period; they had simply not bothered to follow the general current westwards, clinging on to a very commodious flat that had originally been acquired by the maternal grandfather, M. Feuillas, a stockjobber on the Bourse in the lush years of the Third Republic before 1914, and a sufficiently well-known figure in the Quartier de la Bourse to have been the subject of several caricatures—bowler hat, spats, long black coat with velvet collar—by famous caricaturists of the turn of the century.

The flat, which was, as I have said, very large, was shaped like an L, with a balconied salon, its two french windows facing on to the boulevard. This room was very seldom used; its furniture, much of the time, was kept under beige covers. There was also a balconied dining-room, round-fronted with a sort of *vue plongeante*, a view from above, right up the boulevard Bonne-Nouvelle past the Bains Neptuna as far as the Théâtre du Gymnase and the Théâtre Sarah Bernhardt. There was a very dark hall which always needed artificial light, and a tiny kitchen facing on to the deep well formed by seven storeys of enclosed *appartements*. Also always lit by electric light was a long, gloomy corridor off which were four bedrooms, themselves equally dark, as only a few feet separated their windows from the tall mass of the building housing the swimming-baths.

The furniture of the salon and of the dining-room, of *faux Louis XVI*, looked as if it had been mostly acquired in one go as a series of sets: *salle à manger, complète*; *entrée, complète*; *chambre à coucher, complète*. And right down to the last detail: *service de table*, several sets of linen, even the bound volumes of the appropriate *grands auteurs*, certainly not designed to be read, but rather to furnish.

Probably, it had all been acquired at the time of Mlle Feuillas' marriage, a suggestion that seemed to be confirmed by the paucity of the kitchen equipment, hinting at a period of purchase many years before the Bazar de l'Hôtel de Ville, the paradise for kitchen-ware, as far as Paris is concerned, angling for the family unit, began to place the chief emphasis on *la femme au foyer*, and to make its reputation in the furnishing of *les arts ménagers*. When Mlle Feuillas married, the kitchen was still the unvisited prison of the maid, who was exhibited professionally only when she was waiting at table, in her best black silk with white apron.

Later, at Samois-sur-Seine, the village on the Seine where the family had a country house, I discovered something like thirty years of the annual catalogues of the Bon Marché, all of them pre-1914, so my guess would be that the family's furniture, with everything that went with it, had been acquired in a bulk order from that emporium when the young stockjobber and his bride had first set up house.

Certainly, there was little to suggest, in the standard parade of marble-topped tables, wall brackets, and so on, any evidence of personal choice or fantasy. Even the Chinese silk screens looked as though they would have gone with the rest, suggesting a date when Pierre Loti was beginning to seep down to the all-inclusive, regimented tastes of the Bon Marché or of the Grands Magasins du Louvre.

The whole set had seen much better days: the silk screens were torn in innumerable places and, in the salon, most of the arm-rests on the chairs were liable to fall off under the slightest pressure. The bookcases, as I soon discovered, were not designed to be opened. I did manage to prise one of them open, whereupon the whole front came away, revealing, along with the bound Hugos and Balzacs, several bound sets of *Le Petit Journal Illustré*. The chairs themselves were quite safe, but scarcely comfortable.

On the other hand, the silver and table service were both heavy and lavish, and the napkins were the size of the towels in which schoolboys would carry their bathing-trunks to the municipal baths. The glassware was reassuringly abundant, and the dinnertable, when fully laid out, made a very fine late-nineteenth-century showing indeed, under an elaborate cluster of electric lights, which sprouted luxuriantly, like oranges, and were held up by rather dusty, gilt-painted cherubs. There was very little doubt as to what constituted the focal point of an *appartement* that still preserved plenty of mainly unused *signes de grandeur*—fitted corner cupboards, stacked with tureens and flowered plates, much of the ugliest and most massive Sèvres, cut-glass, and fruit-knives.

The maid slept somewhere above the seventh storey, somewhere under the roof, though she seemed to be on call any time from 7.30 a.m. until midnight, save on Saturday afternoons, when she went out with her fiancé, who was a young Alsatian, like herself.

The family had remained in the boulevard Bonne-Nouvelle as a sort of bourgeois enclave in an encroaching sea of *fourreurs, tapissiers, merciers, rubaniers, bimbelotiers, dentistes américains* who, whatever their origin, were certainly not American. Many of the tenants, as far as I could make out, did not live on the premises, but simply used the flats as workshops, returning at night to rooms in the *XIme*, *XIIme* or the *IVme arrondissements*. Certainly, at night, the *cage d'escalier* was eerily quiet and one never met anyone coming up or going down after about 8 p.m.

The two sons, however, made up for the surrounding silence and stillness by a maximum amount of noise and bustle, taking the stairs at a furious gallop, and endlessly telephoning their friends, male and female, groping for the Bottin in the pitch-black hall, feebly lit by an anaemic yellowish bulb, to the west and south-west of the city (they had quite a few in the *VIIme*, some among the parishioners of Sainte-Clothilde, rather more in the *VIIIme* and the *XVIme*, or in the far-away Ternes, with cousins, the children of Madame Thullier's artistic sister and a massive barrister, in Saint-Mandé). Édouard was beginning his P.C.B. at the Faculty of Medicine; François was preparing to set up in the Hôtel Drouot, as a *commissaire-priseur*, and was thus running through the dreary hoops of a *licence de droit*. Perhaps it was on account of the latter's destined career that they had thus held on to a quarter given over more and more to offices, chain stores, vast cafés, and cinemas, and, in the *passages*, alleyways, *cités*, and small streets to the north of the Boulevard, small trades: engravers, printers of visiting cards and *faire-parts*, manufacturers of rubber stamps (by no means a declining industry), sign-painters, stamp-traders, and very small haberdashers.

They were the nearest thing to Parisian one was ever likely to encounter. Both sides of the family had originated from the Seine-et-Marne, first as peasants, then as speculators in national lands; and Madame Thullier still possessed rural properties—a whole street of houses in the Brie, a house in the valley of the Seine, land in that of the Bièvre. But they were rude about most provincials, referred to peasants as *les pecquenots*, employed, often quite unconsciously, a great deal of Paris slang, particularly when describing women and girls: '*bien fringuée*', '*toute pomponnée*', '*de jolies châsses*', and that sort of thing—some of it acquired, I suppose, in hospital wards, much of it also from the shop-girls whom they ran after at week-ends—and possessed an outsize packet of Parisian cheek, particularly well employed by François, once he had become established as an auctioneer, his iron voice brilliantly accompanied by his *aboyeurs*: a veritable orchestra in the long vowels of common Parisian. They were certainly not of a philosophical bent, were not given to pure speculation, were never heard to formulate a general idea or theory, were only peripherally interested in politics, but much engaged in football and in chasing girls, of all conditions, though only French ones: they were quite immune to the exoticism and mystery of *l'âme slave*, preferring a typist from Belleville or Bezons any day, though a Russian accent in French sent them off in peals of laughter. Not for them either the smoky delights of *la peau mate* or *les blondeurs* of the Nordics; in fact, they were remarkably unadventurous in this respect, though, much later in life, when he was a doctor with the French Army in Indochina, Édouard seems / to have widened his interests. Although they had been to L'École des Roches as boarders, they did not appear to have even a disapproving awareness of homosexuality, and the standard French jokes about antique dealers and dress designers did not figure in their repertoire. There was then a certain innocence about them even in the totally uninhibited cheek that they displayed in the pursuit of shop-girls or merely female fellow-travellers on *les trans-*

ports communs. In this one respect at least I felt myself considerably more worldly-wise than these two hardened and joyful *dragueurs* (there was too a strong element of competitiveness in their sweeping, as in everything else, save, of course, Law and Medicine). They also attached a considerable importance to the joys of eating and drinking; but this certainly did not extend to good behaviour at table; on the contrary, the more important the guests, the worse would be their behaviour. They enjoyed being students, rather than studying, and were complete extroverts. They were sentimental, foolhardy, and potentially very brave. Their courage was not just juvenile *panache*: in 1939, the lawyer volunteered for the Corps Francs, and was probably one of the few soldiers thoroughly to have enjoyed the period of the phoney war, which, for him, was anything but, consisting of almost daily *coups de main* against German outposts in the forêt de Warndt; the doctor remained behind, in sole charge of a large military hospital, somewhere in the area of the Maginot Line, in June 1940, and was captured by the Germans. In 1935, my own fear was that they would kill us all there and then: themselves, their mother, the maid, and myself, as a result of the utterly reckless manner in which they drove Madame Thullier's enormous black Panhard-Levassor, on the week-end trips to Samois-sur-Seine.

Although they made rude remarks about peasants, they were also given to boasting about their peasant ancestors—great-grandparents and so on—no doubt as enhancing their own rise to the level of a solid and affluent professional bourgeoisie. They did not often talk about money; but there always seemed to be plenty of it. Clearly, apart from landed and urban property, *le père* Feuillas must have left a substantial fortune in the safer shares. They were certainly not the sort of people who would have fallen in a big way for Russian bonds: *chemins de fer* and *la Rente* were their mother's declared stand-bys.

Both boys much looked forward to the prospect of war, though they did not have any strong ideas as to whom it should be against. As their father had been killed at Gallipoli, they tended on the whole to stick to the Entente system of alliances, mainly out of a sense of family loyalty. But I think that they would have most favoured the Italians as ideal enemies, as they could see themselves giving them a sound trouncing; also *les Ritals* were ridiculous, and their rendering of French represented one of the brothers' favourite party-pieces late on a convivial evening; though I never heard them express any views of Fascism, Ciano was one of their most cherished butts, because he rolled his eyes and brilliantined his hair (they always referred to him as '*le gommeux*'). In fact, *all* Italians were objects of high comedy. Hitler certainly was not that; but he might not have existed, as far as they were concerned, for I cannot recall his name ever having been mentioned in No 26, though they had a number of Austrian friends. But they were apt to make rude remarks about Jews, and were also given to imitations of Jewish furriers, old-clothes-merchants, and so on, as they attempted to wrestle with the ambiguities of French. I do not think, however, that they were truly anti-semitic, it was not so positive as that. Pretty well *anyone* with a foreign accent in French was something of a joke-figure, though none could compete with '*les macaronis*'. There were others within France, too, mostly Marseillais and other southerners, and Bécassine and other female simpletons (*gourdes*) from where she came from in the depths of *la Bretagne breton-nante*.

They also possessed a considerable repertoire of anti-papal and anti-clerical songs and stories. There was one sung saga about the adventures of a Paris prostitute who, repentant, '*est allée voir le Pape à Rome*', finding him, predictably, in a brothel. They regarded priests as poor, hybrid creatures, skirted men who did not serve any useful function in life and were driven to take sex surrep-titiously (they claimed to have a detailed knowledge of the specialised clerical brothels in the Quartier Saint-Sulpice). I suspect that their most vigorous and scandalous manifestations of anti-clericalism were directed at their mother, whom they greatly loved and indeed, in important matters, respected, but whose totally non-religious attachment to the proprieties of the religious calendar and to very occasional attendance at Mass they easily saw through. In fact, they were no fools, and were quick to detect pretension and hypocrisy, reserving their very worst manners for the occasional visits to dinner of the various literary and artistic luminaries, some of them aspiring *académiciens*, none actually immortalised—not even later on, which was surprising, such was their common mediocrity—most of them of the long-winded and eloquent sort that one would associate with Alliance Française lectures or with fashionable *conférences* in the Faubourg-Saint-Honoré, who represented Madame Thullier's claim to intellectual status. They were genuinely proud of her artistic achievements and of the of-ficial recognition that she had received, as Présidente de la Société des Femmes-Peintres, from la Ville de Paris, the arms of which, *fluctuat*, *mergitur*, the *Nef*, and the rest, she wore, on such occasions, as an outsize medal pinned on her dress like a *camée*. They also thought, rightly, that her painting, and her standing with *les femmes-peintres*, kept their mother occupied and reasonably happy. They were good sons. But they had little time for intellectuals, male or female; and I never saw either of them, or Madame Thullier, read a book, whether a novel or the sort of fashionable history dished out by la Maison Hachette.

The brothers were not, however, total philistines, regularly attending each new play at l'Atelier, and having a special admiration for Dullin himself. There was a good deal of theatre—or should it be music-hall?—about their own noisy manner of life, even the simplest gestures being accompanied by the most almighty clatter; and I have never met anyone who derived more genuine pleasure from the sound of breakage, especially that of china or glass, a pleasure which I entirely shared with them, so that I offered a most appreciative audience, and I think the amount of breakage much increased in my time.

I have always believed that François chose the career of *commissaire-priseur* as much for the opportunity it offered him to cut a wonderfully eloquent public figure, from the moment that he made a very rapid and businesslike *entrée* on his rostrum, plunging straight into the sale, with a semi-serious description of some grotesque object held up before him, as if it had been a heraldic symbol, by two of his uniformed acolytes, and acquiring full momentum in the breakneck *'qui dit mieux?'* of the actual bidding, and exercising his machine-gun repartee at the expense of the most faithful attendants, whom he could pick out at a glance, even if they were standing half-hidden right at the back of his *salle*, at that anarchical cult, as to make a lot of money, which he certainly did as well. Each of his appearances at the Hôtel Drouot represented a small masterpiece of Parisian cheek and knockabout humour, with his audience conquered from the start, and the regulars drawn in by name. He also greatly enjoyed the extensive social promiscuity involved in the job, finding himself completely at home with a disparate group ranging from doubtful *brocanteurs*, Greek philatelists, Armenian carpet-dealers, elderly female eccentrics who spent most of their time nosing around the different *salles*, attending every sale of their favourite, Maître Thullier, and never buying anything—their pleasure was purely artistic—of elegant, fastidious, and thin-waisted antique-dealers, and very rough, ill-spoken *ferrailleurs* and *chiffonniers*, in from the flea markets of the Porte des Lilas and the Porte de Montreuil. He was perhaps the only auctioneer in the place not to have a speciality: carpets, postage stamps, pictures, silver, jewellery, furniture, china, *everything* passed his way, a veritable shower of junk and valuables, the intimacies of past régimes and forbidden, once glorious pleasure-palaces—he put under the hammer a bust of Jean Chiappe, a full-length portrait of Jacques Doriot, standing with his deputy's sash, on a barricade, against a background of red flags, factory chimneys, and clenched fists; at one sale he knocked off, in lots of half a dozen, official photographs of Marshal Pétain, the full uniform of a deceased *immortel* was held up in front of him, commented upon, along with its former wearer, the *bicornes* of *polytechniciens* would be disposed of in company with the shakos of *cyrards*, medals and sashes showered on the table in front of him, immense quantities of female clothing, down to the intimacies of night-wear, knickers, shifts, *soutiens-gorge*, and under-skirts would appear on the anatomical shelves in front of his rostrum, as if this had been an unofficial *morgue*, minus the bodies, with the *clothes* desparately seeking their lost owners, and, in the immediate wake of the *loi Marthe-Richard*, it fell to him to dispose of the entire stock of two of the most celebrated Paris brothels, right down to the erotic lamp-stands and priapic bathroom fittings: a challenge to his descriptive powers which he met with comfortable brilliance, amidst a perfect uproar of hilarity.

His office in the nearby rue Rossini, a sort of antechamber to the real drama, looked as if it had been contrived to the specifications of Salvador Dali. Like, so it is said, the last Emperor of Germany, he affected to receive customers while seated on a rocking-horse or any other bizarre mount that had come his way, including elaborately decorated commodes or massively gothic ecclesiastical furniture; and he seemed to expand in the menacing company of springing tigers and panthers, growling leopards, cheetahs with holes in them and the stuffing coming out, bored-looking owls, and a jaded stuffed pike, *aux yeux glauques*, drinker's eyes as boiled as those of one of his *aboyeurs*.[1] Indeed, I suspect that he secretly

[1] In Pagnol's delightful *La Gloire de mon père* (1957) there is the description of the varied contents of the shop of a *bougnat* (*vins charbons*) in Marseilles before the First World War: '. . . des remparts d'armoires, des miroirs lépreux, des casques, des pendules, des bêtes empaillées . . . ce robinet col de cygne, *nickelé par galvanoplastic* . . . ce tam-tam de la Côte d'Ivoire . . . un immense drapeau de la Croix-

preferred *le toc* to the real thing, the fancifully hideous extravaganza, of no conceivable use, to the object of rare beauty and great value; and that he liked to live with objects that were bizarre and big, grimacing and in awful colours, as a sort of perpetual student engaged in an everlasting *Bal des Quatz'Arts*, a carnival that for him took place thrice daily, three days a week. He threw himself into his sales, his wild performances on the rostrum, spectacularly aided by his choir of *aboyeurs*, whose muscles were as strong as their stentorian Parisian voices, with a frenetic energy worthy of Pierre Brasseur acting *Kean*. But he was alone on the stage, a one-man act, in which every gesture, every *coup d'oeil*, every inflexion of the voice was used to maximum effect. No wonder his audience seldom varied; few enough came to buy, a great many came merely to watch, and to be spotted and called out by name.

It was not just the public performance. He enormously enjoyed the haggling, even if it was over some wretched broken telephone, a chair with a leg missing and the seat giving way, or a family photograph album. He spent much of his time chatting with the odd creatures who brought in their daily haul of impossible objects, and was extremely friendly to such a minor operator as my oldest French friend, Maurice Chauvirey. Perhaps, even more, his occasional *voyages à l'intérieur* took him out of the daily round of dust, noise, and flotsam; entry into closed apartments, to make an inventory of furniture, silver, china, linen, the truly astonishing interiors of elderly recluses: bachelor or spinster couples, survivors of noble lineages, shut away in the Faubourg Saint-Germain, for thirty or forty years, the light penetrating into a fortress closed and shuttered for as long, the ghastly, pathetic, or comical secrets of families gradually unfolding before the washed-out blue, rather globular eyes—his eyes were strikingly like those of the Bourbons—of the auctioneer, the unbelievable smells of old age, avarice, neglect, loneliness, total sloth. Here was a man who had little need to travel, and who could have written, many hundreds of times, *Voyage à travers ma chambre*, save that, better still, each time it would always be someone else's. He liked the *aristos*

Rouge . . . un billet mauve de cinquante francs . . . ,' some of the débris, washed up on the Mediterranean shore, and ending up high up in the city, far from the port, indicative of the importance of Marseilles as a *dépôtoir* of the colonial trade. And a very visual reminder of the changes of period and régime as represented by the altering colours of banknotes, mauve taking one back to the *belle époque*.

best—not out of any *bourbonien* affinity or political sympathy, but
because their raped interiors were much more unpredictable,
always much filthier, often with layers and layers of dirt, and their
contents much more bizarre than in the apartment of a banker or
an Inspecteur des Finances, where everything would be neat and in
place. He had a theory that some elderly *marquises* and *vicomtesses*
must have kept themselves in trim well into their eighties by hurling
the heads of deer and moose across the room or throwing Sèvres set
pieces at one another. He enjoyed the evidence of such posthumous
breakage as much as he had enjoyed smashing things, as a young
man, when I first met him, No 26, his mother's much-misused flat.

On reflection, I think François was a committed artist, a poet,
even a social historian of a kind, endlessly fascinated by breaking
into privacy and totting up the balance-sheet of lonely, hidden, and
unambitious lives. His favourite customers were those who never
bought anything and from whom he never obtained a commission,
who came to the Hôtel like gamblers to the green tables, because
they had nothing else to do, because they lived in a fantasy world
which he helped to create for them. He was not an indifferent man;
and his fascination with useless objects came from his own deep
humanity, he was not so much interested in the objects as such, but
in the people, mostly dead, to whom they had at one time been attached and to whom they had once given pleasure. His curiosity
about people was insatiable; and I suppose he will go on in the
Hôtel Drouot till he drops, for there is no retiring age in that
profession. I have come to understand why he has never felt the
urge to read a novel, or even follow the *chronique judiciaire* in a
newspaper. It is all there in his *salle* on the second floor: his theatre,
his full expression, his realisation, to which his chaotic office in the
rue Rossini is a *loge*, a place of preparation, meditation, conversation, and, sometimes, rest.

With his brother, a quieter, less flamboyant person, medicine
eventually satisfied very different needs. Édouard preferred the
quiet parts, away from the limelight, finally setting up as a con-
sultant anaesthetist, on call night and day, as well as in general
practice, Boulevard Malesherbes, on the fringes of an upper-class
and a lower-middle-class quarter, offering then a varied clientèle.
He was the silent man, the watcher, the giver of sleep. When I first
met them, the two boys seemed to have much in common, François
being so overpowering that something of him ran off onto his
younger brother. But I think Édouard was only making a show of

trying to keep up with the spanking pace set by his ebullient elder. Once separated, they developed quite differently, and while François grew in size and in noise and clamour, his brother disappeared to the Far East, only returning at his mother's entreaty. Even so, and though both married, they remained very close. They were in fact very fond of each other and came, in later years, to appreciate one another's differences. Édouard spoke with amused affection of his brother's extraordinary performances on the rostrum. What they did have in common—and retained together—was immense physical courage, a marvellously juvenile irreverence—I had come to the right place early to learn the sense of *épater le bourgeois*—an apparently limitless capacity for enjoyment in such important matters as food, drink, girls, and, as far as François was concerned, in that, related, of war, seen indeed as a sort of prolongation of sport, and a great deal of generosity. Public affairs and politics passed largely beside them, with only muted echoes at No 26.

The *Xme arrondissement*, as far as I know, possesses no literature, and it has been sung about by no poet. Could it be that people simply walk through it in haste to work, in fatigue at the end of the day, along the regular east-west itinerary described in one of Raymond Queneau's novels, *Le Chiendent*, or noisily hitting this outdated *voie triomphale* of music, vice, and pleasure, all three of very low quality, on Saturday nights? As if, indeed, it were but a *lieu de passage*, a sort of surface Métro, just like the one following exactly the same route, reflecting the same street intersections, just below the ground. I wonder.

Yet lovers must have met on its broad pavements, domestic dramas dragged along its grim, Sunday expanses, friendships been born between prostitutes and clients on the corner of the rue Faubourg Montmartre or in the little café opposite the Porte Saint-Denis.

It was not murder country. That was farther north: Pigalle, Place Blanche, La Chapelle. Or it was farther east: in the old, traditional badlands of the rue de Lappe and 'La Bastoche'. Or it was over on the other side of the river, along the deserted *quai* skirting the Jardin des Plantes. Pigalle and 'La Bastoche', in particular, still attempted to disguise themselves as dangerous territory, certainly convincingly enough to make the tourist on a tour of the *bals musettes* shiver in anticipation of the knives coming out. Nor was it really *faits divers* country, save for the occasional street accident,

though I know that suicide often briefly inhabited its loneliness in
small hotels situated in side-streets like the rue Mazagram—*voie
sans issue*.

For me at least, the *Xme arrondissement* still holds the freshness
of relative innocence, of adolescence, and, above all, of discovery
and acclimatisation, so, perhaps, I am the one who should com-
memorate it: part of central Paris witnessed both from the fifth
floor and at boulevard and Métro level. One's home station offers
as warmly welcoming a homecoming, as great a sense of belonging,
as a return from any familiar itinerary which is regularly followed.
For me, the famous *agent à double barbe*, the man who had a huge
beard coming down into two points, who was always on traffic
duty in the daytime at the Porte Saint-Denis, signified the imminence of lunch or dinner. And I could even recognise the man
who sold *Paris-Soir* in the long corridor of the Métro Bonne-
Nouvelle, intoning like a litany, in a voice of monotonous despair,
as if the last thing he wanted was ever to sell one of his papers,
'*Paris-Soir . . . l'Intran . . . Sport*,' with a voice falling in a sort of
death agony on the last word, as if it signified ultimate doom,
rather than Longchamps, Vincennes, Compiègne, and Chantilly,
the Vélo d'Hiv and the Palais des Sports, Roland-Garros, and
Colombes.

I went to sleep to the tired, dawdling sound of the Métro heading
unhurriedly towards Faubourg Montmartre and Richelieu-Drouot
or the bustling Strasbourg-Saint-Denis. I could distinguish between
the wheezing gears of the green bus and the sound of a private car,
and I woke to the noise of many heels walking rapidly to work on
the wooden boulevard. It was as good an introduction, I think, as
one could wish for, offering very few constraints and certainly absolutely no pretensions.

If, indeed, the *Xme arrondissement* has produced any literature,
it would not be in French; it would more likely be in Yiddish—a
chronicle of lost *Stetl* and of dispersed families from White Russia,
Lithuania, Poland, and Rumania, populations decimated by the
Second World War. I walked up the dark and musty staircase of No
26 sometime late in the 1960s and could find no Polish, Russian, or
Rumanian names any more, only the names of Armenian carpet-
dealers and of dentists.

And yet it was a district of Paris as much deserving of literature
as the fashionable literary quarters of Paris or those patronised by
populist writers—Ménilmontant, Belleville, or La Goutte-d'Or.

The glass *passages* behind the boulevard Bonne-Nouvelle are as bizarre as those enclosed journeys in glass-covered surrealism explored so lovingly by Aragon, in *Le Paysan de Paris*, in the 1920s, farther west in the Quartier de la Bourse and the Quartier Saint-Lazare. And for sheer ugliness and monumental bad taste, the monster cheap clothing stores that line the street between Bonne-Nouvelle and Richelieu-Drouot must surely be *hors concours*, at least in the highly competitive terms of purely Parisian ugliness.

The quarter, then, would seem to have been crying out for literary commemoration of the same imaginative sympathy and careful observation as two recent works of that great Paris historian, Louis Chevalier, *Les Parisiens* and *L'Assassinat de Paris*, both of them evocations of a Paris which, as he says, is *le paradis perdu*—a Paris already largely lost.

List of Authors, Works, and
Persons Referred to in the Text

Ajar, Émile (pseudonym of Pierre Petrovich)
  La Vie devant soi (Prix Goncourt, 1974)
Alain-Fournier (pseudonym of Henri-Alban Fournier), 1886-1914
  Le Grand Meaulnes (1913)
Allio, René, born 1924, film director
  La Vieille Dame Indigne (film 1965)
Ambrière, Francis, born Paris 1907
  Les Grandes Vacances 1939-1945 (1946)
Aragon, Louis, born Paris 1897
  Le Paysan de Paris (1926)
Aron, Raymond, born Paris 1905
  (with André Labarthe) ed. *La France Libre* (monthly, London, 1940-44)
d'Astier de la Vigerie, Emmanuel, born Paris 1900
  Sept fois sept jours (1947)
  L'Eté n'en finit pas (1945)
  De la Chute à la libération de Paris (1965)
Aymé, Marcel, born Joigny, 1902-1967
  La Jument verte (1933)
  Le Vin de Paris (1947)
  La Tête des autres (1952)

Bainbridge, Beryl, born 1934
  A Quiet Life (1977)
Barbusse, Henri, 1873-1935
  Le Feu (Prix Goncourt, 1916)
Barrès, Maurice, 1862-1923
  Les Déracinés (1897)
Bazin, Hervé (Jean-Pierre Hervé-Bazin) born Angers 1911
  Vipère au poing (1948)
  La Mort du petit cheval (1950)
Bazin, René, 1853-1932
  Les Oberlé (1901)
  Le Blé qui lève (1907)
de Beauvoir, Simone, born 1908
  Les Mandarins (Prix Goncourt, 1954)
Benjamin, René, born Paris, 1885-1948
  Dans les Pas du Maréchal (1942)
Béraud, Henri, born Lyons 1885, died Île-de-Ré 1958
  Le Martyre de l'obèse (Prix Goncourt, 1922)
  La Gerbe d'or (1928)
Bernard, Marc, born Nîmes 1900
  Une Journée toute simple (1950)
Besnard, Marie (*née* Marie-Joséphine-Philippine Davailland), born 15 August 1896
  Saint-Pierre-de-Maillé (Vienne)
  Les Mémoires de Marie Besnard (1962; English translation 1963)

Blakiston, Noel, born 1905
    Collected Stories (1977)
Böll, Heinrich Theodor, born Cologne 1917
    The Train Was on Time (English translation 1973)
    And Where Were You, Adam? (English translation 1973)
    Children Are Civilians Too (short stories, English translation 1973)
Bordeaux, Henri, 1870-1963
    Les Roquevillard (1906)
Bory, Jean-Louis, born Méréville 1919
    Mon Village à l'heure allemande (Prix Goncourt, 1945)

Cagayous, le Journal de, satirical weekly in *pied-noir* slang published in Algiers
    (Belcour), c. 1890 − c. 1935.
Camus, Albert, born Algiers 1913, killed 1960
    L'Étranger (1942)
Canard Enchaîné, le, satirical political weekly founded in 1916 and published in
    Paris
Céline, Louis-Ferdinand (pseudonym of Dr. Destouches), born Paris 1894, died
    Meudon 1961
    Voyage au bout de la nuit (1932)
    Mort à crédit (1936)
    D'un château l'autre (1957)
Cendrars, Blaise (pseudonym of Frédéric-Louis Sanser), born la Chaux-de-Fonds
    1887, died 1961
    Moravagine (1926)
    L'Homme foudroyé (1945)
    La Main coupée (1946)
Chevalier, Louis, born 1911, historian of Paris
    Classes laborieuses et classes dangereuses (1958) (republished in 'Livre de Poche',
    with *avant-propos* by Richard Cobb, 1978)
    Les Parisiens (1967)
    L'Assassinat de Paris (1977)
Chevallier, Gabriel
    Clochemerle (1934)
    Sainte-Colline (1937)
Cocteau, Jean, 1889-1963
    Thomas l'imposteur (1923)
Colette, Sidonie-Gabrielle, 1873-1954
    Le Blé en herbe (1923)
Conchon, Georges, born Saint-Avit 1925
    L'État Sauvage (1964)
de Coster, Charles Théodore Henri, born Munich 1827, died 1879
    *La Légende et les Aventures héroiques, joyeuses et glorieuses d'Ulenspiegel et de
    Lamme Goedzak au pays de Flandre et ailleurs* (1867)
Courteline, Georges (pseudonym of Georges Moineaux), 1858-1929
    Le train de 8h. 47 (1888)

Dabit, Eugène, born Montmartre 1891, died Sebastopol 1936
    Hôtel du Nord (1929)
    Petit Louis (1930)
    Faubourgs de Paris (1933)
    Un Mort tout neuf (1934)
Darien, Georges (pseudonym of Georges-Hippolyte Adrien), born Paris, 46 rue du
    Bac, 1862, died Paris 1921
    Bas les coeurs! (1890; Pauvert, 1957)

Biribi (1890; Martineau, 1966)
Le Voleur (1900; Pauvert, 1955)
La Belle France (1900; Pauvert, 1965)
Daudet, Alphonse, born Nîmes 1840, died Paris 1897
  Lettres de mon moulin (1866)
  Tartarin de Tarascon (1872)
  Numa Roumestan (1881)
Dékobra, Maurice, born Paris 1888
  La Madone des sleepings (1925)
Descaves, Lucien, 1861-1949
  Sous-offs (1887)
Dorgelès, Roland (pseudonym of Roland Lecavelé), **born Amiens, 1886-1973**
  Les Croix de bois (1919)
Drieu la Rochelle, Pierre-Eugène, 1893-1945
  Gilles (1939)
Duclos, Jacques, 1896-1975, Communist politician
  Mémoires (1968-73)
Dullin, Charles, 1885-1949, actor and director of the Théâtre de l'Atelier, Paris, 1922-40
Duprat, Jacques (pseudonym: Léopold van Swavenhaage)
  Le 6 décembre (1965)
Duras, Marguerite (*née* Marguerite Donnadieu), born Gia Dinh, Indochina 1914
  Un Barrage contre le Pacifique (1950)
  Moderato Cantabile
Durban, François (pseudonym of Robert Wibaux)
  Rüdig (1926)
Dutourd, Jean, born 1920
  Au Bon Beurre (1952)
Duvivier, Julien, born Lille, 1896-1967, film director
  Carnet de bal (film, 1937)

Elgey, Georgette, born 24 February 1929, historian
  La Fenêtre ouverte (1973; English translation 1974)
Escartefigue, Marius-Charles-André, born Marseilles, 1872-1957, Socialist politician in Toulon in the 1900s
Etcherelli, Claire, born 1934. Pupille de la Nation.
  Élise ou la Vraie Vie (Prix Fémina, 1967)
Exbrayat, Charles (Charles Hubert Exbrayat-Durivaux), born Saint-Étienne 1906, Lyonnais detective-story writer
  Méfie-toi, gône (1961)
Expilly, l'abbé Jean-Joseph, 1719-1793
  Dictionnaire géographique, historique, et politique des Gaules et de la France (1762-70)

Fallet, René, born Villeneuve-Saint-Georges 1927
  Banlieue sud-est (1947)
Fargue, Léon-Paul, 1876-1947
  Le Piéton de Paris (1939)
Fourcade, Marie-Madeleine, born Marseilles 1909, *résistante*
  L'Arche de Noë (1968)

Galtier-Boissière, Jean, born Paris 1891
  Mémoires d'un Parisien (1960)
Gary, Romain, born Tiflis 1914
  Éducation européenne (1943)

Genet, Jean, born Paris 1910
    Notre-Dame des Fleurs (1942)
Giono, Jean, born Manosque 1895, died there 1970
    Regain (1930)
    Que ma joie demeure (1935)
Gravier, Jean-François, born 1915
    Paris et le désert français (1947)
Grenadou, Éphraïm, born 1897
    (with Alain Prévost, 1930-71) *Grenadou, paysan français* (1966)
Guilloux, Louis, born 1899
    La Maison du peuple (1927)
    Le Sang noir (1935)
    Le Jeu de patience (1949)
Guimard, Paul, born 1921
    Rue de Havre (1957)
    L'Ironie du sort (1961)
    Les Choses de la vie (1967—film 1970 directed by Claude Saulet)
Guingouin, Georges, F.T.P. Resistance leader in the Haute-Vienne, *député-maire* of
    Limoges 1945
Guiral, Pierre, born Marseilles 1909, historian of Marseilles
    Libération de Marseille (1974, preface by Gaston Defferre)

'Hansi' (pseudonym of Jean-Jacques Walz), born Colmar 1873, died 1951
    Le Professeur Knatschke (1912)
Hardy, René, *dit* Didot, *résistant*
    L'Affaire Hardy
Hermant, Abel, 1869-1950
    Le Cavalier Miserey 21me Chasseurs (1899)

Istrati, Panaït, born Braïla 1884, died Bucharest 1935
    Oncle Anghel (1924)
    Kyra Kyralina (1924)
    Codine (1926)

Jardin, Pascal, born 1934
    *La Guerre à neuf ans: une histoire de Vichy par un Saint-Simon en culottes
    courtes* (1972; English translation 1974)

Kessel, Joseph, born Argentina 1898, died 1979
    L'Équipage (1923)
    L'Armée des ombres (1946)
Kirst, Hans Hellmut, born 1914
    La Révolte du Caporal Asch (French edn. 1955)
Koestler, Arthur, born Budapest 1905
    Scum of the Earth (1941)

Labarthe, André, born Paris 1902
    (with Raymond Aron) ed. *La France Libre* (monthly, London, 1940-44)
Larbaud, Nicolas Valery, born Vichy 1881, died there 1957
    Fermina Marquez (1911)
    Enfantines (1918)
Larguier, Léo, 1879-1950
    Saint-Germain-des-Prés mon village (1976)
Le Roy Ladurie, Emmanuel, born 1929, historian
    Histoire du Languedoc (1962)

Les Paysans de Languedoc (1966)
Montaillou (1975)
Le Carnaval de Romans (1979)

MacOrlan, Pierre (pseudonym of Pierre Dumarchey), 1882-1972
Quai des Brumes (1927)
La Tradition de minuit (1930)
Marceau, Félicien (pseudonym of Louis Carette), born Cortemberg, Belgium, 1913
Bergère légère (1953)
Les Élans du coeur (1955)
Creezy (Prix Goncourt, 1972)
Masson, Loÿs, born Mauritius 1915, died 1969
Le Notaire des noirs (1961)
de Maupassant, Guy, 1850-93
Boule de suif (1880)
Mademoiselle Fifi (1882)
Mauriac, François, 1885-1970
Thérèse Desqueyroux (1927)
Monnier, Henri, 1799-1877
L'Enterrement
Morand, Paul, 1888-1976
Fermé la nuit (1923)

Neave, Airey, born 1916, murdered 1979
Saturday at MI9 (1969)
Nizan, Paul, born 1905, killed 1940
Antoine Bloyé (1933)
La Conspiration

Pagnol, Marcel, 1895-1974
Topaze (1928)
Marius (1929)
Fanny (1932)
César (1936)
Merlusse (film, 1934)
La Gloire de mon père (1958)
Le Château de ma mère (1960)
Le Temps des secrets (1960)
Le Temps des amours (1977)
Perret, Jacques, born 1903
Bande à part (1951)
La Bête Mahousse (1951)
Petiot, Dr. Marcel, born 1897, mass murderer of the period 1940-43, with one of
his consulting rooms in the rue esueur; tried, and guillotined in Paris 5.00 a.m.,
25 May 1946
Peyrefitte, Roger, born Castres 1907
Les Amitiés particulières (1944)
La Mort d'une mère (1950)
Manouche (1972)
Philippe, Charles-Louis, 1874-1909
Bubu de Montparnasse (1901)
Poirot-Delpech, Bertrand, born Paris 1929
Le Grand Dadais (1958)
de Pourtalès, Guy, born Geneva
La Pêche miraculeuse

Queffélec, Henri, born Brest 1919
    Journal d'un salaud (1944)
Queneau, Raymond, born Le Havre 1903, died Paris 1976
    Le Chiendent (1933)
    Un Rude Hiver (1939)
    Pierrot mon ami (1942)
    Loin de Rueil (1945)
    Le Dimanche de la vie (1952)
    Zazie dans le métro (1959)

Radiguet, Raymond, 1903-1923
    Le Diable au corps (1923)
    Le Bal du comte d'Orgel (1924)
Ramuz, Charles-Ferdinand, 1878-1947
    Vie de Samuel Belet (1913)
    L'Histoire du soldat (1916)
Rebatet, Lucien, 1903-72
    Les Décombres (1943)
Renoir, Jean, 1894-1978, film producer, director, and writer
    La Marseillaise (film, 1939)
Restif de la Bretonne, Nicolas-Edme, 1734-1806
    Le Paysan perverti ou les Dangers de la ville (1775)
    La Paysanne pervertie (1776)
    Les Contemporaines (1780-85)
Rhys, Jean, 1894-1979
    The Wide Sargasso Sea (1966)
Roblès, Emmanuel, born Oran 1914
    Les Hauteurs de la ville (1948)
    Le Vésuve (1961)
    La Croisière (1968)
Romains, Jules (pseudonym of Louis Farigoule), 1885-1972
    Mort de quelqu'un (1911)
    Les Copains (1913)
    Knock ou le Triomphe de la médecine (comedy, 1923)
    Les Hommes de bonne volonté (1932-47)
Roy, Jules, born Rovigo, Algeria, 1907
    La Vallée heureuse (1946)
    Le Navigateur (1955)
    Les Chevaux du soleil (1968)

Sagan, Françoise (pseudonym of Françoise Quoirez), born 1935
    Bonjour Tristesse (1954)
    Un Certain Sourire (1956)
    Aimez-vous Brahms? (1959)
de Saint-Pierre, Michel (Michel de Grosourdy, marquis de Saint-Pierre), born Blois 1916
    Les Aristocrates (1954)
Sarrazin, Albertine, born Algiers 1937, died 1967
    La Cavale (1965)
    L'Astragale (1965)
    La Traversière (1966)
Sarrazin, Julien, born Amiens
    Contrescarpe (1975)
Sartre, Jean-Paul, born Paris 1905
    La Nausée (1938)

Kean (1954)

Serge, Victor (pseudonym of Victor Lvovich Kibalchick), born Brussels 1890, died Mexico City 1947
Mémoires d'un révolutionnaire (1952; English translation 1963)

Simenon, Georges, born Liège, Belgium, 1903
Cécile est morte (1940)
Au Bout du rouleau (1947)
L'Enterrement de M. Bouvet (1950)
La Mort de Belle (1952)
Le Veuf (1959)
La Mort d'Auguste (1966)
Le Déménagement (1967)

Simonin, Albert
Le Petit Simonin Illustré

Sue, Eugène (Marie-Joseph Sue), 1804-57
Les Mystères de Paris (1842-3)

Sullerot, Évelyne, born Montrouge 1924
Simenon (Éditions Francis Lacassin et Gilbert Sigaux, 1972)

Supervielle, Jules, born Saint-Jean-Pied-du-Port, 1884, died 1960
Le Voleur d'enfants (1926)
L'Enfant de la haute mer (1931)

Thibaudeau, Antoine Claire, comte de
Mémoires sur la Convention et le Directoire (1824)
Mémoires sur le Consulat (1827)

Thomas, Edith, died 1971, historian
Rossel (1967)

Timmermans, Félix, 1886-1947
Pallieter (1916)

Tournier, Michel, born Paris 1924
Le Roi des aulnes (Prix Goncourt, 1970)
Vendredi ou la Vie sauvage (1973)
Les Météores (1975)

Vailland, Roger, 1907-65
Drôle de jeu (1945)
La Truite (1964)

van der Meersch, Maxence, born in Roubaix 1907, died 1951
Maria: fille des Flandres (1935)
Invasion 1914 (1935)
L'Empreinte de Dieu (1936)

Vercors (pseudonym of Jean Bruller), born 1902
Le Silence de la mer (1942)

Vidalenc, Jean, historian
L'Exode (1956)

Waugh, Evelyn, 1903-66
Decline and Fall

Zeldin, Theodore
France 1848-1945, two vols. (1973 and 1975)

Zola, Émile, 1840-1902
La Terre (1887)

Index of Names

Index of Place Names